AL-FĀDĀNĪ'S
TREATISE ON LOGIC

AL-FĀDĀNĪ'S TREASTISE ON LOGIC

رسالة في علم المنطق

Risālah fī ʿilm al-manṭiq

Shaykh Muḥammad Yasīn al-Fādānī

Translation & notes by

MUSA FURBER

ISBN   978-1-944904-23-4 (paper)

Published by:
Islamosaic
islamosaic.com
publications@islamosaic.com

All praise is to Allah alone, the Lord of the Worlds
And may He send His benedictions upon
our master Muhammad, his Kin
and his Companions
and grant them
peace

TRANSLITERATION KEY

ء ' (A distinctive glottal stop made at the bottom of the throat.)

ا ā, a

ب b

ت t

ث th (Pronounced like the *th* in *think*.)

ج j

ح ḥ (A hard *h* sound made at the Adam's apple in the middle of the throat.)

خ kh (Pronounced like *ch* in Scottish *loch*.)

د d

ذ dh (Pronounced like *th* in *this*.)

ر r (A slightly trilled *r* made behind the upper front teeth.)

ز z

س s

ش sh

ص ṣ (An emphatic *s* pronounced behind the upper front teeth.)

ض ḍ (An emphatic *d*-like sound made by pressing the entire tongue against the upper palate.)

ط ṭ (An emphatic *t* sound produced behind the front teeth.)

ظ ẓ (An emphatic *th* sound, like the *th* in *this*, made behind the front teeth.)

ع ʿ (A distinctive Semitic sound made in the middle of the throat and sounding to a Western ear more like a vowel than a consonant.)

غ gh (A guttural sound made at the top of the throat, resembling the untrilled German and French *r*.)

ف f

ق q (A hard *k* sound produced at the back of the palate.)

ك k

ل l

م m

ن n

ه h (This sound is like the English *h* but has more body. It is made at the very bottom of the throat and pronounced at the beginning, middle, and ends of words.)

و ū, u

ي ī, i, y

ﷺ A supplication made after mention of the Prophet Muhammad, translated as "May Allah bless him and grant him peace."

CONTENTS

المُحْتَوَيَاتُ

FOREWORD

In the name of Allah the Most Merciful and Compassionate

When my doctoral student Musa Furber presented me with his translation of Shaykh Muḥammad Yasīn al-Fādānī's *Risālah fī ʿilm al-manṭiq,* I recognised immediately what a service it could render. The *Risālah* occupies a particular niche in the classical tradition: it is introductory without being superficial, rigorous without being forbidding. Al-Fādānī composed it for "novices"—his own word—who needed a ladder into the science, and he structured it as a series of questions and answers precisely because that format strips away the intimidating apparatus that can make classical *manṭiq* texts so impenetrable to beginners. The Arabic original achieves its purpose admirably. The question was whether an English translation could do the same.

Muḥammad Yasīn al-Fādānī (1335–1410 AH / 1917–1990 CE) requires little introduction to those already acquainted with twentieth-century Islamic scholarship. Born in Mecca to a Sumatran scholarly family of some distinction, he rose to become one of the foremost authorities on hadith in the Arabian Peninsula, eventually serving as supervisor and director of Dār al-ʿUlūm al-Dīniyyah. He was a prolific author whose writings span hadith, jurisprudence, Arabic, astronomy, and logic. The *Risālah fī ʿilm al-manṭiq* reflects the clarity of mind and pedagogical sensitivity that characterised his teaching. It is also a text with deep roots in the region: al-Fādānī's family came from the Nusantara world, his works are read and taught in traditional circles throughout the archipelago, and it is precisely this living familiarity with the text that makes it a natural choice for an institution such as the International Islamic University of Malaysia, whose students are themselves predominantly from the region.

I had taught this course previously using a different introductory work, but found it wanting in ways that were difficult to work around in a classroom setting—both in its handling of technical terminology and in the reliability of the English it produced. When Furber's translation became available, I adopted it in its place. I have since used it as the assigned introductory text on three occasions at the International Islamic University of Malaysia between 2023 and 2025. Each time the course was offered, I reviewed the translation with the students in hand—working through the text, identifying passages where the English could be tightened, where a technical term required more precise handling, or where an additional note would assist readers without prior grounding in the Islamic sciences. That process, repeated over three successive cohorts, constitutes in effect a sustained peer review of the work in classroom conditions—one that affords a degree of confidence in the translation that one rarely obtains from reading a manuscript in isolation. The feedback received at each iteration has made the work more reliable and more teachable than it would otherwise have been.

Al-Fādānī composed his *Risālah* so that students might enter the study of *uṣūl al-fiq*h and *balāghah* with a sound grounding in *manṭiq*. That aim is no less pertinent for English-speaking students of the Islamic sciences today, and this translation makes it available to them in a way that no prior English rendering of the text has managed. I hope it serves its readers as well as it has served my students.

ASSOC. PROF. DATO' DR. MUHAMMAD AYMAN AL-AKITI
DEPARTMENT OF USUL AL-DIN & COMPARATIVE RELIGION & PHILOSOPHY
AHAS KIRKHS
INTERNATIONAL ISLAMIC UNIVERSITY MALAYSIA
16 RAMADAN 1447 AH/5 MARCH 2026 CE

TRANSLATOR'S PREFACE

In the name of Allah the Most Merciful and Compassionate

This booklet presents a translation of Shaykh Muḥammad Yasīn al-Fādānī's (1335–1410 AH/1917–1990 CE) *Risālah fī ʿilm al-manṭiq* (*Treatise on Logic*).

The *Risālah* opens with the ten foundational principles (*mabādiʾ*) that classical scholars prefaced to any science—most importantly, in this case, the definition of manṭiq, its subject matter, its relation to other sciences, and the legal ruling for studying it. This is followed by the essential epistemology: the nature of originated knowledge (*ʿilm ḥādith*), its division into necessary (*ḍarūrī*) and speculative (*naẓarī*), and the fundamental bipartition of knowledge into conceptualisation (*taṣawwur*) and assent (*taṣdīq*), which provides the organisational framework for everything that follows. The first main division treats conceptualisations (*taṣawwurāt*), covering utterances and their classifications, the five universals (*kulliyyāt khams*), and definitions (*taʿrīfāt*); the second treats assents (*taṣdīqāt*), covering propositions (*qaḍāyā*), conversion (*ʿaks*), and syllogism (*qiyās*) together with its figures, moods, and materials (*mawādd*). The author presents the material in a question-and-answer format, which he adopted deliberately to lower the barrier of entry for students with no prior exposure to the science. No background in *manṭiq* is assumed, though familiarity with basic Arabic grammatical terminology is helpful. The text sits above the very shortest primers—it covers more ground and with greater elaboration than, say, al-Abhārī's *Īsāghūjī*—but well below intermediate works such as al-Taftāzānī's *Tahdhīb*; it is best understood as preparation for those works, and for the logical vocabulary that pervades the *mutūn* of *uṣūl al-fiqh* and *balāghah*. The author states this purpose plainly in his own preface. A student who works through the *Risālah* carefully should be able to proceed to *uṣūl al-fiqh* and *kalām* (such as al-Bayḍāwī's *Minhāj* or al-Taftāzānī's *Sharḥ al-ʿAqāʾid*) without being impeded by unfamiliar terminology, and will have the foundations needed to advance to a more substantial *manṭiq* text.

ABOUT THE AUTHOR

The author of the text comes from a family of scholars hailing from Padang, West Sumatra, though he himself was born in Mecca in 1355/1917. He began his studies with his father, Shaykh Muḥammad ʿĪsā al-Fādānī, and his uncle, Shaykh Maḥmūd al-Fādānī. He then enrolled in the Madrasah al-Ṣawlatiyyah al-Hindiyyah. While there, he also attended lessons in al-Masjid al-Ḥarām. He also studied at Dār al-ʿUlūm al-Dīniyyah in Shiʿb ʿAlī, Mecca, once it had been established. During his various studies, he gathered many chains of narration and became the hadith authority of Mecca. He taught at Dār al-ʿUlūm al-Dīniyyah, where he was appointed its supervisor and director. He held those positions until passing away in 1410/1990.

He authored hundreds of books and treatises on hadith, jurisprudence, Arabic, astronomy, and logic—including our text.

ABOUT THE TRANSLATION

The Arabic text of this translation is based on Maṭbʿah Dhī Yūnītīd's undated third edition. I have taken some liberties with the English titles (such as adding numbers) and have converted some paragraphs to number or bullet lists.

The footnotes are of three kinds. Notes prefaced "Al-Fādānī:" are the author's own, present in the Arabic original; they elaborate on points in the main text, and in particular flag divergences between the usage of the logicians (*manāṭiqah*) and that of the scholars of *uṣūl al-fiqh (uṣūliyyūn)*—which, given the author's stated purpose, are often the most instructive notes in the book. Notes prefaced "(Tr:)" are the translator's, addressing matters of translation, terminology, or context relevant to English-speaking readers. Unmarked footnotes are also the translator's work; they supply source identifications for persons and texts mentioned in the main text or in the other notes. The author's notes are strongly recommended and should be read alongside the main text; the translator's notes—both the marked and unmarked ones—are supplementary and may be set aside by readers who prefer to focus on the text itself.

I translated this text during the second half of August 2022 as a quick review of logic. I have hastily revised and printed it at the request of Dr Muhammad Ayman al-Akiti. Many thanks are owed to him and the individuals who reviewed drafts of the translation and offered corrections, encouragement, and advice. Last but not least, I owe much to my wife and children for their constant support and sacrifice over the years.

* * *

May Allah bless the author of the text, those mentioned in the text or footnotes, those who contributed in any way to bringing it to English readers, and their fellow readers. And may He forgive the translator and protect readers from his copious shortcomings.

MUSA FURBER
CYBERJAYA, MALAYSIA
1447 AH/2026 CE

AL-FĀDĀNĪ'S TREATISE ON LOGIC

رسالة في علم المنطق

Risālah fī ʿilm al-manṭiq

AUTHOR'S PREFACE

مقدِّمةُ المؤلِّفِ

بِسمِ اللَّهِ الرَّحمَنِ الرَّحيمِ

الحمدُ للَّهِ ربِّ العالمينَ، والصلاةُ والسلامُ على سيِّدِنا محمّدٍ أشرفَ المرسَلينَ، وعلى آلِه وصحبِه أجمعينَ.

أمّا بعـدُ: فهـذه رسـالةٌ لطيفـةٌ فـي علـمِ المنطقِ على طريقِ السؤالِ والجـوابِ، جمعتُهـا لتكونَ بمثابةِ سُـلَّمٍ لإخواني المبتدئينَ في تفهُّمِ الكتـبِ المتداولةِ في هذا العلـمِ، وعَوناً لهم على الدخـولِ في علمَي أصولِ الفقهِ والبلاغةِ.

واللَّهَ أسألُ أن يعمَّ بها النفعَ، آمينَ.

In the name of Allah the Most Merciful and Compassionate

Praise be to Allah, Lord of the World. Supplications and peace be upon our master Muḥammad the noblest of messengers, and upon his household and companions in [their] entirety.

To commence: This gentle treatise concerning the science of logic (*manṭiq*) follows a question-and-answer format. I compiled it to serve as a ladder for my brethren who are novices to [ascend and thereby gain access to] the currently circulating books on this science and to facilitate their entering into the sciences of principles of jurisprudence (*uṣūl al-fiqh*) and rhetoric (*balāghah*).

Allah [alone] I ask to spread its benefit. *Amīn.*

1

THE PRINCIPLES OF THE SCIENCE OF

LOGIC

مبادئُ علمِ المنطقِ

س   ما هو علمُ المنطقِ؟

ج   هو علمٌ يُبْحَثُ فيه عن المعلوماتِ التصوُّريّةِ والتصديقيّةِ مِن حيثُ
إنَّها تُوَصِّلُ إلى مجهولٍ تصوُّريٍّ أو تصديقيٍّ.

Q   What is the science of logic?

A   It is a science wherein where conceptual (*taṣawwuriyyah*) and
assertoric (*taṣdīqiyyah*) knowns are studied in terms of them
arriving at a conceptual or assertoric unknown.

س   ما موضوعُه؟

ج   المعلوماتُ التصوُّريّةُ والتصديقيّةُ مِن حيثُ إيصالِها إلى مهجولاتٍ.

Q   What is its subject?

A   [Its subject is] conceptual and assertoric knowns inasmuch as
them arriving at unknowns.

س   مَن واضعُه؟

ج   هو أرِسطاطاليس مِن الحكماءِ.

Q   Who is its founder?

A   Aristotle,[1] one of the philosophers (*ḥukamā'*).

س   ما اسمُه؟

ج   هو علمُ المنطقِ، ويُسمّى أيضًا بـ «الميزانِ» و «مِعْيارِ العلومِ».

Q   What is its name?

A   It is the *science of logic* (*'ilm al-manṭiq*). It is also called the *scale* (*al-mīzān*) and the *standard for sciences* (*mi'yār al-'ulūm*).

س   ما استمدادُه؟

ج   مِن العقلِ.

Q   What are its sources?

A   The intellect.

س   ما غايتُه؟

ج : هي عصمَةُ الإنسانِ عن أن يَضِلَّ فكرُه في العلومِ.

Q   What is its purpose?

A   It[s purpose] is protecting the individual from his reasoning about sciences become misguided.

س   ما حكمُ تعلُّمِه؟

---

1   Aristotle, the Ancient Greek philosopher and polymath (384–322 BC). His *Prior Analytics* is credited with being the earliest study of formal logic. It, along with his *Categories, On Interpretation, Posterior Analytics, Topics,* and *On Sophistical Refutations* were posthumously compiled into set of six books known as *Organon* (meaning "instrument"). In the Arab world, his *Rhetoric* and *Poetics* were appended to these six.

ج   فيه تفصيلٌ، وهو أنَّ:

١.   مــا ليــسَ مخلوطًا بكفريَّاتِ الحكماءِ كهذه الرسالةِ ليسَ في
جــوازِ الاشــتغالِ بـه خلافٌ، بـل فرضُ كفايةٍ علـى أهلِ كلِّ
إقليمٍ؛ لأنَّه يتوقَّفُ عليه ردُّ الشكوكِ وشُبَهِ المبتدعةِ وهذا فرضُ
كفايةٍ،

٢.   وأمَّا ما كانَ مخلوطًا بكفريَّاتِهم ففيه أقوالٌ ثلاثةٌ:

أحدُها لابنِ الصلاحِ والنوويِّ أنَّه يَحرُمُ،

وثانيُها للغزاليِّ أنَّه يجوزُ، قالَ: «مَن لا يَعرِفُه لا يُوثَقُ بعلمِه»،

وثالثُها -وهو القولُ المختارُ-(٢) أنَّه يجوزُ لمَن وَثِقَ مِن نفسِه بصحّةِ
ذِهنِه ومارسَ الكتابَ والسنّةَ.

Q   What is the legal ruling (ḥukm) for learning it?
A   It is detailed.
1.   What is not mixed with the disbeliefs of the philosophers
(ḥukamāʾ)—like this treatise—: there is no disagreement
concerning the permissibility of occupying oneself with
it. Indeed, it is a communal obligation (farḍ kifāyah) for
the people of every region since rebutting the doubts and
delusions of innovators—which is a communal obligation—depends upon it.
2.   What is mixed with their disbeliefs [i.e. of the philoso-
phers]: there are three opinions:

---

٢   هذا القول مأخوذ من قول الشيخ تقي الدين السبكي لما سئل عنه: ينبغي أن يقدم على الاشتغال
به الاشتغال بالكتاب والسنة والفقه، فإذا رسخ في الذهن تعظيم الشريعة ولقي شيخا حسن
العقيدة فهو من أحسن العلوم وأنفعها في كلّ بحث، وكان هذا القول مختارًا؛ لجمعه بين
القولين الأولين.

The first [opinion] (that of Ibn al-Ṣalāḥ[3] and al-Nawawī[4]) is that it is unlawful.

The second (that of al-Ghazālī[5]) is that it is permissible. He [Imām al-Ghazālī even] said, "Whoever does not know it [logic]: his knowledge is not reliable."

The third (the preferred opinion[6]) is that it is permissible for whomever has trust in the soundness of his intellect and practices [according to] the Quran and Sunnah.

---

3   'Uthmān ibn 'Abd al-Raḥmān ibn 'Uthmān, Abū 'Amr Ibn al-Ṣalāḥ (d. 643) was a great Shafi'ī legist and hadith scholar. He served as a teacher at Dār al-Ḥadīth in Damascus, where he dictated what has become one of the classic manuals on hadith sciences.

4   Yaḥyā ibn Sharaf al-Ḥūrānī al-Nawawī, Abū Zakariyā (631–676) was the great Imam of Shāfi'i fiqh and hadith, known for his piety and asceticism. He authored several books.

5   Muḥammad ibn Muḥammad ibn Muḥammad ibn Aḥmad, Abū Ḥāmid al-Ghazālī, *Hujjat al-Islām* (450–505) was an eminent Shāfi'ī legist, Sufi, and theologian. His works include *Iḥyā 'ulūm al-dīn, Tahāfūt al-falāsifa, Mi'yār al-'ilm, Al-Muṣṭaṣfā fī 'ilm uṣūl al-fiqh, Al-Wasīṭ, and Al-Iqtiṣād fī al-itiqād*.

6   Al-Fādānī: This opinion is taken from what Sheikh Taqi al-Dīn al-Subkī said when asked about it: One should prioritise engaging with the Quran, the Sunnah, and jurisprudence. Once veneration of the Sharī'ah is firmly established in the mind and one encounters a teacher with sound creed, then it is among the best and most beneficial sciences in every inquiry. This opinion is preferred because it combines the first two opinions.

2

ORIGINATED KNOWLEDGE AND ITS

CLASSIFICATIONS

العلمُ الحادثُ وتقسيماتُه

س   ما هو العلمُ الحادثُ؟

ج   هــو معرفـةُ المعلــومٍ^(٧)، وبعبارةٍ: هــو مُطلــقُ الإدراكِ، وأُخرى: هو حصولُ صورةِ الشيءٍ في النفسِ.

Q   What is *originated knowledge* (*'ilm ḥādith*)?[8]

A   It is knowing of something that is known (*ma'lūm*).[9]
    An[other] expression is that it is absolute perception.
    Another is that it is obtaining the representation of a thing in
    the intellect.

---

٧   جميع هذه التعاريف اصطلاح المناطقة، إلا أن التعريفين الأخيرين يشملان الجهل المركب، وأما عند الأصوليين فهو: إدراك خاص، أي: حكم الذهن الجازم المطابق لموجب من حس أو عقل أو عادة، وهذا المعنى لا يقبل الانقسام المذكور هنا.

8   (Tr:) "originated" (*ḥādith*) refers to that whose existences is preceded by
    non-existence.

9   Al-Fādānī: All of these definitions are terminology of the logicians, except
    that the last two definitions encompass *compound ignorance* (*al-jahl al-mu-
    rakkab*). However, according to the scholars of principles of jurisprudence
    (the *uṣūlīs*), it is a specific perception, i.e. the firm judgment of the mind that
    corresponds to reality due a necessitating sensory, intellectual, or customary
    factor. This meaning does not accept the division mentioned here.

7

س   ما الفرقُ بينَ العلمِ والمعلومِ؟

ج   لا فـرقَ بينَهمـا إلّا بالاعتبارِ، فالصورةُ باعتبارِ حصولُها في النفسِ تُسمّى «علمًا»، وباعتبارِ حصولِها في الخارِج تُسمّى «معلومًا».

Q   What is the difference between knowledge (*'ilm*) and what is known (*al-ma'lūm*)?

A   There is no difference between them except in perspective. The apprehended image (*ṣūrah*) from the perspective of its occurrence in the intellect is called *knowledge* (*'ilm*), and from the perspective of its external occurrence is called *what is known* (*ma'lūm*).

س   إلى كَمْ يَنقسمُ العلمُ الحادثُ؟

ج   يَنقسمُ إلى قِسمَينِ: علمٌ ضروريٌّ[10]، وعلمٌ نَظَريٌّ.

Q   Originated knowledge (*'ilm ḥādith*) divides into how many divisions?

A   It has two divisions:
   1.   necessary knowledge (*'ilm ḍarūrī*),[11] and
   2.   speculative knowledge (*'ilm naẓarī*).

---

١٠   قد يفرق بينهما: بأن العلم الضروري يقع بقدرة اللّه غير مقدور للعباد، بخلاف النظري فإنه مقدور للعباد بالقدرة الحادثة عند الأكثرين، هذا ويؤخذ من تقسيم العلم إليهما أن العلوم الحادثة بعضها ضروري وبعضها نظري، وهو القول الأصح؛ إذ لو كان جميعها ضروريا لما جهلنا شيئا أو كان جميعها نظريا لدار وتسلسل، والدور والتسلسل كلاهما محال.

11   Al-Fādānī: The two may differentiated by stating that *necessary knowledge* (*'ilm ḍarūrī*) occurs by the will of Allah and is not within the control of the servants, whereas *speculative knowledge* (*'ilm naẓarī*) is within the servants' capacity by the ability, according to most. From dividing knowledge into these two categories, it can be understood that some of the originated sciences are necessary and some are speculative, which is the soundest view. For if all of them were necessary, we would know nothing, or if all of them were speculative, it would lead to circular reasoning and an infinite regress, both of which are absurd.

2. KNOWLEDGE

س   ما هو العلمُ الضروريُّ؟

ج   هـو مـا يَحصُـلُ بغيرِ نظـرٍ، كتصـوُّرِك وجـودَك وكإدراكِ أنّ الواحدَ نصفُ الاثنَينِ.

Q   What is *necessary knowledge* (*'ilm ḍarūrī*)?

A   It is what occurs without speculation (*naẓar*). Such as you conceptualising your existence and your awareness that one is half of two.

س   ما هو العلم النظريُّ؟

ج   هـو مـا يحصلُ بنظرٍ، كتصـوُّرِ حقيقةِ الإنسـانِ وكإدراكِ أنّ العالَمَ حادثٌ.

Q   What is *speculative knowledge* (*'ilm naẓarī*)?

A   It is what occurs through speculation (*naẓar*). Such as conceptualising the true nature (*ḥaqīqah*) of a person. And such as your awareness that the world is originated.

س   ما هو النظرُ؟

ج   هـو الفكـرُ في حـالِ المنظورِ فيه لتُعرَفَ حقيقتُـه أو ليُعلَمَ أو يُظَنَّ حكمُه.

Q   What is *speculation* (*naẓar*)?

A   It is pondering the state of the object being speculated (*manẓūr fīhi*) in order that its true nature become known, or to know or to assume its ruling (*ḥukm*).

س   ما شرطُ النظرِ الصحيحِ؟

ج   يُشترطُ له ثلاثةُ أُمورٍ:

الأوّلُ: العقلُ،

والثاني: انتفاءُ أضدادِ النظرِ مِن الغفلةِ والتقليدِ وفسادِ الإعتقادِ،

والثالـثُ: أن يقـعَ النظرُ مِـن الجهةِ التي مِن شأنِهـا أن ينتقلَ الذهنُ بها إلى المطلوبِ.

Q   What are the conditions of sound speculation (*naẓar ṣaḥīḥ*)?
A   It has three conditions.
The first is reason (*'aql*).
The second is negating the contraries of speculation (*aḍdād al-naẓar*), including inattention, emulation, unsound belief.
The third is that the speculation occurs in a manner which moves the mind to the sought after [conclusion].

س   إلى كَمْ يَنقسمُ العلمُ باعتبارِ مُتَعَلَّقِهِ؟

ج   يَنقسمُ إلى قسمَينِ: تصوّرٌ وتصديقٌ (١٢).

Q   Knowledge (*'ilm*), with respect to its connection, divides into how many divisions?
A   It has two divisions:
    1.   conceptualisation (*taṣawwur*), and
    2.   assent (*taṣdīq*).[13]

---

١٢   من هذا التقسيم يظهر لك أن الأشياء التي يتعلق بها العلم نوعان: «تصورية وتصديقية»: فالنوع الأول: إما أشخاص: وهذه لا تعرف إلا بطريق التحليل وهو عبارة عن تجزئة الشخص، كمعرفة هذه الرسالة، وهذا البيت، وقد تركه متأخرو المناطقة في كتبهم. وإما أنواع: وهي تعرف بطريق المعرفات، ومبادئها الكليات الخمس، كمعرفة حقيقة الإنسان، والتقسيم مساعد في هذين الطريقين؛ لأن به تعرف الأجناس والأنواع والفصول وهكذا. والنوع الثاني: الأجناس -أعني: الأحكام- وهذه لا تعرف إلا بالأقيسة، ومبادئها القضايا. فانحصر مبحث هذا العلم في أربعة: - مبادئء التصورات: وهي الكليات الخمس. ومقاصد التصورات: وهي المعرفات. ومبادئء التصديقات: وهي القضايا. - ومقاصد التصديقات: وهي الأقيسة.

13   Al-Fādānī: From this division, it becomes clear to you that the things related to knowledge are of two types: (1) *conceptual* (*taṣawwurī*), and (2) *assertoric* (*taṣdīqī*).

س ما هو التصوّرُ؟

ج هـو إدراكُ ماهيّةِ الشـيءِ مِـن غيرِ حكمٍ عليهـا بإثبـاتٍ أو نفيٍ،
كإدراكِ حقيقةِ الإنسانِ وهي «حيوانٌ ناطقٌ» مِن غيرِ حكمٍ عليهِما
بشيءٍ.

Q   What is a *conceptualisation* (*taṣawwur*)?

A   It is perceiving a thing's quiddity (*māhiyyah*) without any
affirmative or negative assertion (*ḥukm*) about it. Such as
perceiving a person's true nature (which is "rational animal")
without asserting anything about the two.

س ما هو التصديقُ؟

ج هـو نفسُ الحكـمِ -أعني (١٤): إدراكَ أنّ النسبـةَ الكلاميّـةَ واقعةٌ أو
ليست بواقعةٍ-، والتصوّراتُ الثلاثةُ -أعني: تصوّرَ الموضوع، وتصوّرَ
المحمولِ، وتصوّرَ النسبةِ الكلاميةِ-، شروطٌ له (١٥) خارجةٌ عنه.

The first type are either

(a) *Individuals* (*ashkhāṣ*): These are known only through analysis (*taḥlīl*), which consists of decomposing the individual, such as knowing this message or this house. This was abandoned by the later logicians in their books.

Or (b) Types: These are known through *definientia* (*muarʿrrifāt*); their foundational principles are the five universals, such as knowing the true reality of "human being."

Division assists in these two methods because through it, genera, species, and differentiae are known, and so on.

The second type [of things related to knowledge] are genera, by which I mean *judgments* (*aḥkām*), and these are known only through syllogisms; their principles are propositions.

Thus, the inquiries in this science are confined to four areas: (1) the principles of conceptions, which are the five universals; (2) the goals of conceptions, which are the identifiers; (3) the principles of assents, which are the propositions; and (4) goals of assents, which are the syllogisms.

١٤ هذا أعني جعل الحكم إدراكا هو التحقيق، وذهب بعض متأخري المناطقة إلى أن الحكم فعل من أفعال النفس.

١٥ هذا عند الحكاء، فيكون التصديق عندهم بسيطا، وقال الإمام الرازي: التصورات الثلاثة أجزاؤه، فيكون التصديق عنده مركبا من أربعة أجزاء «التصورات الثلاثة، والجزء الرابع هو الحكم».

Q   What is an *assent* (*taṣdīq*)?

A   It is the assertion (*ḥukm*) itself (meaning:[16] conceptualising
that the verbal relationship exists or does not exist).
The three conceptualisations (*taṣawwurāt*)—meaning:
1.   conceptualising the subject (*mawḍūʿ*),
2.   conceptualising the predicate (*maḥmūl*), and
3.   conceptualising the verbal relationship (*nisbah*)
—are conditions for it[17] [which are] external to it.

س   إلى كَمْ يَنقسمُ^(١٨) التصديقُ؟

ج   يَنقسمُ إلى أربعةِ أقسامٍ: يقينٌ، وظنٌّ، وجهلٌ مركَّبٌ، وتقليدٌ.

Q   Assent (*taṣdīq*) divides[19] into how many divisions?

A   It has four divisions:

---

16   Al-Fādānī: This, meaning the consideration of judgment as a form of com-
prehension, is the accurate view. Some later logicians, however, held that
assertion is one of the actions of the soul.

17   Al-Fādānī: This is according to the philosophers (*ḥukamāʾ*), so assent for
them is simple. Imām al-Rāzī, however, said that the three conceptions are
its components, making assent for him composed of four parts: the three
conceptions, and the fourth part is the assertion.

١٨   على هذا التقسيم يكون التصديق أحد قسمي العلم، وهذا عند المناطقة. وأما عند
الأصوليين: فالعلم قسم من أقسام التصديق حيث قالوا: إن التصديق «بمعنى الحكم»
ينقسم إلى: ١. حكم جازم لا يقبل التغير فيسمى: «علمًا». ٢. وحكم جازم يقبل التغير
فيسمى: «اعتقادًا». ٣. وحكم غير جازم فيسمى: «ظنًّا»، ٤. وحكمين يتقاوم سببها
فيسمى: «شكًّا».

19   Al-Fādānī: According to this division, assent is one of the two types of
knowledge; this is the view of the logicians. However, for the scholars of
foundations of jurisprudence (the *uṣūlīs*), knowledge is a type of assent,
since they said that assent, in the sense of assertion, is divided into:

(1) a firm assertion (*ḥukm jāzim*) that does not accept change, which is
called *knowledge* (*ʿilm*);

(2) a firm judgment that accepts change, which is called *belief* (*iʿtiqād*);

(3) a non-firm judgment, which is called *speculation* (*ẓann*); and

(4) two judgments whose causes counterbalance each other, called *doubt*
(*shakk*).

1.   certainty (*yaqīn*),
2.   conjecture (*ẓann*),
3.   compound ignorance (*jahl murakkab*), and
4.   emulation (*taqlīd*).

س   ما هو اليقينُ؟

ج   هـو الإعتقـادُ الجـازمُ المطابـقُ الراسـخُ الـذي لا يعرِضُ لـه زوالٌ بتشكيكِ المشكِّكِ.

Q   What is *certainty (yaqīn)*?

A   It is a belief that is held with conviction, corresponds [to reality], and entrenched, which is not susceptible to being removed by a doubter causing doubts.

س   ما هو الظنُّ؟

ج   هو الاعتقادُ الراجحُ سواءٌ طابقَ أو لم يُطابق.

Q   What is *conjecture (ẓann)*?

A   It is the preponderant belief, whether or not it corresponds [to reality].

س   ما هو الجهلُ المركَّبُ؟

ج   هو الاعتقاد الجازمُ الغيرُ مطابقٍ.

Q   What is *compound ignorance (jahl murakkab)*?

A   It is a belief held with conviction and does not match reality.

س   ما هو التقليدُ؟

ج   هو الاعتقادُ الجازمُ المطابقُ الغيرُ الراسخِ.

Q   What is *emulation* (*taqlīd*)?
A   It is a belief held with conviction that matches reality, which is not entrench.

2

UTTERANCES AND THEIR

CLASSIFICATIONS

اللَفظ وتَقسيماتُهُ

س إلى كَمْ يَنقسمُ اللفظُ؟

ج يَنقسمُ إلى قسمَينِ: مستعمَلٍ، ومُهمَلٍ.

Q   *Utterances* (*alfāẓ*, pl. of *lafẓ*) divide into how many divisions?
A   They divide into two divisions:
  1.   operational (*mustʿmal*) and
  2.   neglected (*muhmal*).

س ما هو اللفظُ المستعمَلُ؟

ج هو اللفظُ الدالُّ على معنىً، ويُسمّى المعنى «مَدلولًا» و «مُسمًّى».

Q   What is an *operational utterance* (*lafẓ mustaʿmal*)?
A   It is an utterance signifying a meaning (*maʿnan*). The meaning is called *signified* (*madlūl*) and *named* (*musammā*).

س ما هو اللفظُ المُهمَلُ؟

ج هو اللفظُ الذي لا يكونُ له معنىً، ويُسمّى أيضًا «غيرُ مستعمَلٍ»، نحوُ: «دَيْزٍ»[20].

---

٢٠   مقلوب «زيد».

Q   What is a *neglected utterance (lafẓ muhmal)*?

A   It is an utterance that does not have a meaning. It is also called *inoperative (ghayr musta'mal)*. Such as "Dayz."[21]

س   إلى كَمْ يَنقسمُ المستعملُ؟

ج   يَنقسمُ إلى قسمَينِ: مُفرَدٍ، ومُرَكَّبٍ.

Q   The operational utterance (*lafẓ musta'mal*) divides into how many divisions?

A   It has two divisions:
   1.   simple (*mufrad*) and
   2.   compound (*murakkab*).

س   ما هو المفردُ؟

ج   هو ما لا يدلُّ جُزؤُه على جزءٍ معناهُ، وهو أربعُ حالاتٍ:

١.   لا يكونُ له جزءٌ كـ «قِ» عَلَمًا،

٢.   له جزءٌ لا معنى له كـ «خالد» علمًا،

٣.   له جزءٌ ذو معنىً ولا يدلُّ على جزءٍ معناه كـ «عبدِ اللَّهِ» علمًا،

٤.   له جزءٌ دالٌّ على جزءٍ معناه لكن لا مِن حيثُ جزؤُه كـ «حيوانٍ ناطقٍ» علمًا لإنسانٍ.

Q   What is a *simple operational utterance (lafẓ musta'mal mufrad)*?

A   It is one whose part does not signify part of its meaning.
   It has four states:
   1.   It does not have a part. Such as "*Qi!*" as a definite noun.
   2.   It has a part which is meaningless. Such as "Khalid" as a definite noun.

---

21   Al-Fādānī: The reversal of "Zayd."

3. It has a part which has meaning but does not signify a part of its meaning. Such as "'Abd Allāh" as a definite noun.

4. It has a part signifying part of its meaning but not as being its part. Such as "a rational animal" as a definite noun for a [specific] human.

س ما هو المركَّبُ؟

ج هو ما يدلُّ جزؤُه على جزءٍ معناه مِن حيثُ إنّه جزؤُه، وهو أنواعٌ:

مِنهـا: المركَّبُ التقييـديُّ، نحـوُ: «حيـوانٌ ناطقٌ»، وهـو المفيدُ لاكتسابِ العلومِ التصوُّريّةِ؛ لأنّه في قُوَّةِ المفردِ،

ومِنهـا: المركَّـبُ الخَبَـريُّ، نحوُ: «الإنسـانُ ناطـقٌ»، وهو المفيدُ لاكتسابِ العلومِ التصديقيّةِ.

Q   What is a *compound operational utterance* (*lafẓ mustaʿmal murakkab*)?

A   It is one whose part signifies part of its meaning, inasmuch as it is its part. It is of several types, including:
   — The *restricted compound operational utterance* (*lafẓ mustaʿmal murakkab taqyīdī*). Such as "rational animal." It is beneficial for acquiring knowledge related to concepts since it has the strength of a simple operational utterance (*lafẓ mustaʿmal mufrad*).
   — The *declarative compound operational utterance* (*lafẓ mustaʿmal murakkab khabariyyah*). Such as " human is rational being." It is beneficial for acquiring knowledge related to assents.

س إلى كَمْ يَنقسمُ المفردُ باعتبارِ استقلالِه؟

ج يَنقسمُ إلى ثلاثةِ أقسامٍ: حَرفٍ، واسمٍ، وفِعلٍ.

Q   The *simple operational utterance*, with respect to its independence, has how many divisions?

A   It has three divisions:
1. particle (*ḥarf*),
2. noun (*ism*), and
3. verb (*fiʿl*).

س   ما هو الحرفُ؟

ج   هو ما لم يستقلَّ بالمفهوميّةِ بأن احتاجَ فيها إلى انضمامِ غيرِه إليه ويُسمّى أيضًا «أداةٌ».

Q   What is a *particle* (*ḥarf*)?

A   It is what cannot be understood on its own in that it needs something else to be joined to it. It is also called an *operand* (*ādāh*)."

س   ما هو الإسمُ؟

ج   هو ما استقلَّ بالمفهوميّةِ ولم يدلَّ على زمانٍ مُعَيَّنٍ.

Q   What is a *noun* (*al-ism*)?

A   It is what is understood on its own without signifying a specific tense.

س   ما هو الفعلُ؟

ج   هو ما استقلَّ بالمفهوميّةِ ودلَّ على زمانٍ معيّنٍ مِن الأزمنةِ الثلاثةِ.

Q   What is a *verb* (*al-fiʿl*)?

A   It is what is understood on its own while signifying one of the three tenses specifically [i.e. past, present, future].

س   إلى كَمْ يَنقسمُ المفردُ باعتبارِ مدلولِه؟

ج   يَنقسمُ إلى قسمَينِ: جُزئيٍّ، وكلّيٍّ.

Q   The simple operational utterance (*lafẓ mustaʿmal mufrad*), with respect to what it signifies, divides into how many divisions?

A   It has two divisions:
1.   particular (*juzʾī*) and
2.   universal (*kullī*).

س   ما هو الجزئيُّ (٢٢)؟

ج   هو ما مَنَعَ نفسُ تَصَوُّرِ مدلولِه مِن أن نَفهَمَ فيه شِرْكَةً كـ «خالد»؛ فإنّ مدلولَه -وهو الذاتُ المُشَخَّصَةُ- إذا تصوَّرَ مَنَعَ ذلك، وكـ «هذا الكرسيُّ» و «هذا البابُ».

Q   What is a *particular simple operational utterance* (*lafẓ mustaʿmal mufrad juzʾī*)?[23]

A   It is that whose very conceptualisation of what it signifies prevents understanding it to have a shared commonality. Such as "Khalid" since conceptualising what it signifies (which is the

---

٢٢   ومن قبيل الجزئي جميع الأعلام الشخصية فإن مدلولها جزئي، ومنه الضمير عند الأكثرين، وقال القرافي: إنه كلي، وقال أبو حيان: إنه كلي وضعا، جزئي استعمالا. وأما علم الجنس كـ «أسامة» فكلي ذهنا ووضعا، جزئي خارجًا، وكلي وجزئي استعالًا؛ لأنه إن كان مستعمَلًا في الحقيقة نحو: «أسامة أجرأ من ثعالة» فكلي، وإن استعمل في فرد منها نحو «هذا أسامة» فجزئي حقيقة إن لوحظ في استعماله الماهية الموجودة في الفرد مجاز في الفرد إن اعتبر الخصوص.

23   Al-Fādānī: Among the particulars are all personal names, as what they signify is particular. This includes pronouns, according to the majority, though al-Qarāfī held that pronouns are universal. Abū Ḥayyān said they are universal in designation but particular in usage. As for a generic name like "Usāmah," it is universal in the mind and in designation, but particular in external reality, and both universal and particular in usage. If it is used in its literal sense, as in "Usāmah is bolder than a fox," then it is universal. But if it is used for an individual, as in "This is Usāmah," then it is particular in reality. If its use emphasises the quiddity present in the individual, it is figurative when considering the specificity.

identified entity) prevents this. And such as "this chair" and "this door."

س   ما هو الكلّيُّ؟[٢٤]

ج   هو ما لم يمنع نفسُ تصوُّرِ مدلولِه مِن أن نفهمَ فيه شركةً، وهو أربعُ حالاتٍ:

١. توجَدُ أفرادُه في الخـارج مُتَناهيّةً، كـ «إنسانٍ»؛ فإنّ مدلولَه -وهو حيوانٌ ناطقٌ- إذا تُصُوِّرَ لم يمنع مِن أن نفهمَ فيه شـركةَ «زَيدٍ» و «عَمرٍو» و «بَكرٍ» واندراجِها تحتَه،

٢. تُوجَدُ أفرادُه في الخـارجِ غيرَ متناهيّةٍ، كـ «نعمةِ اللَّهِ تعالى»،

٣. لـم تُوجَـد في الخـارجِ سواءٌ امتنعـت عقلًا كـ «الجمعِ بينَ الضدَّينِ» أو أمكنت كـ «خيلٍ مِن ياقوتٍ»،

٤. وُجِـدَ مِنهـا فردٌ واحدٌ سـواءٌ امتنعَ وجودُ غيرِه كـ «الإلهِ» أي: المعبودِ بحقٍّ، أو أمكنَ كـ «الشمسِ» أي: الكوكبِ النهاريِّ المُضيءِ[٢٥].

Q   What is a *universal simple operational utterance (lafẓ mustaʿmal mufrad kullī)*?[26]

---

٢٤ ومن قبيل الكلّي النكرات كـ «رجل وفرس» فإن مدلولها كلّي.

٢٥ اعلم أن عندهم ألفاظًا ستة: هي: «كلّي وجزئي، وكلية وجزئية، وكل وجزء»: فاللفظان الأولان هما المذكوران هنا. والكلّية: هي الحكمُ على كل فرد من أفراد العام مطابقة بحيث لا يبقى منه فرد، نحو: «كل رجلٍ يشبعه رغيف أو رغيفان»، ومن قبيلها: جميع صيغ العموم كـ «مَن» و «ما» و «الذي». والجزئية: هي الحكم على بعض الأفراد نحو: «الأستاذ حاضر». والكلّ: هو الحكم على مجموع الأفراد من حيث هو مجموعٌ، نحو: «كل رجل يحمل الصخرة العظيمة» أي: مجموعهم، ومن قبيله: أسماء العدد كـ «العشرة والمائة والألف» فإن مدلولها كل وهو الحكم على مجموع الآحاد من حيث هو مجموع. والجزء: هو ما تركب الكل منه ومن غيره كـ «الخمسة مع العشرين».

26   Al-Fādānī: Among the universals are the indefinite nouns, such as "man" and "horse," for what they signify is universal.

A   It is one whose very conceptualisation of what it signifies does not prevent understanding it to have a shared commonality. It has four states.

1.   Its members (*afrāduhu*) exist in the external world in finite numbers. Such as "human" since conceptualisation of what it signifies (rational animals) does not prevent understanding it having a shared commonality with "Zaid," "'Amr," and "Bakr," and them falling within it.

2.   Its members exist in the external world in infinite numbers. Such as "the blessings of Allah (Most High is He)."

3.   They [its members] do not exist in the external world, whether it is

    a.   impossible according to reason (such as "the combination of two contraries (*ḍiddayn*)"), or

    b.   possible (such as "a horse made of sapphire").[27]

4.   One single member exists, whether others are

    a.   impossible [to exist] (such as "the Deity," i.e. the one truly worshipped), or

    b.   possible (such as "the sun," i.e. the luminous daytime celestial orb).[28]

---

27   Some books have "mountain (*jabal*) made of…" instead of "horse (*khayl*) made of…"

28   Al-Fādānī: Know that they have six phrases: (1–2) universal and particular; (3–4) universality and particularity; and (5–6) whole and part.

The first two terms are what have been mentioned here.

Universality (*killiyyah*) refers to the assertion that applies to every individual of a general category exactly, such that no individual is left out, as in "Every man is satisfied by one or two loaves of bread." Examples of this include all expressions of generality, such as "whoever," "whatever," and "which."

Particularity (*juz'iyyah*) refers to an assertion that applies to some individuals, as in "The teacher is present."

Whole (*kull*) refers to an assertion that applies to the totality of individuals as a collective, as in "All the men are carrying the great rock," meaning the entire group. An example of this is numerical terms such as "ten," "one hundred," and "one thousand," for what they signify is a whole, which is the assertion on the total sum of units as a collective.

س   إلى كَمْ تنقسمُ دلالةُ اللفظِ؟

ج   تنقسـمُ إلى ثلاثةِ أقسـامٍ: دلالـةِ مُطابَقةٍ، ودلالةِ تَضمُّنٍ، ودلالةِ
الالتزامٍ.

Q   The *utterance's signification* (*dalālat al-lafẓ*) divides into how many divisions?

A   It has three divisions:
1.   correspondence signification (*dalālat mutābaqah*),
2.   inclusive signification (*dalālat taḍammun*), and
3.   implicative signification (*dalālat iltizām*).

س   ما هي دلالةُ المطابقةِ⁽²⁹⁾؟

ج   هي دلالةُ اللفظِ على كلِّ موضوعِه، كدلالةِ «إنسانٍ» على «حيوانٍ
ناطقٍ»، ودلالةِ «حائطٍ» و«فرسٍ» على مدلولَيهما.

Q   What is *correspondence signification* (*dalālat al-mutābaqah*)?[30]

A   It is the utterance signifying all of its subject. Such as "human" signifying "rational animal," and "wall" and "horse" [signifying] what they signify.

س   ما هي دلالةُ التضمُّنِ؟

ج   هـي دلالـةُ اللفـظِ على جـزءٍ موضوعِه، إن كانَ له جـزءٌ، كدلالةِ

Part (*juz'*) refers to that from which the whole is composed, along with other parts, as in "five with twenty."

٢٩   ومن قبيل دلالة المطابقة: دلالة العام على أفراده عند الأصوليين كـ «جاء عبيدي»؛ لأن ذلك
في قوة قضايا متعددة بعدد أفراد العام، أي: «جاء فلان، وجاء فلان... وهكذا»، ودلالة كل
قضية منها على مدلولها بالمطابقة فلتكن دلالة ما في قوتها كذلك.

30   Al-Fādānī: Among the types of correspondence signification is the indication of the general term on its specific instances, as in "My slaves came," because this is equivalent to multiple propositions equal to the number of instances of the general term, that is, "So-and-so came, and so-and-so came... and so on." Each of these propositions indicates its meaning through correspondence, so let the signification of the general term be similarly effective.

«إنسانٍ» على «حيوانٍ» فقط وعلى «ناطقٍ» فقط، وكأن يدلُّ على «الحائطِ» بلفظِ «بيتٍ».

Q   What is *inclusive signification (dalālat al-taḍammun)*?

A   It is the utterance signifying a part of its subject (if it has a part). Such as "human" signifying just "animal" and just "rational." And such as signifying "wall" with the utterance "house."

س   ما هي دلالةُ الالتزامِ؟

ج   هـي دلالـةُ اللفظِ علـى أمرٍ خارجٍ عن موضوعِـه مُلازمٍ له، كدلالةِ «إنسانٍ» على «قابلِ العلمِ»، ودلالةِ «أسدٍ» على «شُجاعٍ»، ودلالةِ «سقفٍ» على «بيتٍ».

Q   What is *implicative signification (dalālat al-iltizām)*?

A   It is the utterance signifying something that is external to its subject yet implied by it. Such as "human" signifying "receptive to knowledge," "lion" [signifying] "bravery," and "roof" [signifying] "house."

س   هل يُشترَطُ في الالتزامِ اللُّزومُ الخارجيُّ؟

ج   لا يُشترَطُ فيه قطعًا، لحُصولِ الفهمِ بدونِه، كما في الضدَّينِ؛ فإنّ أحَدَهمـا يُفهَمُ مِـن الآخَرِ بدونِ تلازُمِهما فـي الخارجِ، بل بينَهما تَعانُدٌ فيه.

Q   Is external implication a condition for inclusive signification (*dalālat al-iltizām*)?

A   It is, with certainty, not a condition since understanding occurs without it. Such as what happens with two contraries since one is understood from the other without external implication. Indeed, there is an antagonism between them.

س هل يُشترَطُ في الالتزامِ اللزومُ الذهنيُّ؟

ج نعــم يُشــترَطُ وجـودُه فيـه^(٣١)، أي: متى حصلَ مُسـمّى اللفظُ في الذهنِ حصلَ ذلك اللازمُ مِنه؛ إذ لا فهمَ للمُسمّى بدونِه ولحصولِ اللازمِ بدونِ أن يكونَ الزمنُ قاطعًا بينَه وبينَ المُسمّى الملزومِ.

Q Is mental implication a condition for implicative signification (*dalālat al-iltizām*)?

A Yes, its existence therein is a condition[32] (i.e. whenever what is named by the utterance comes to mind, that *implicative consequence* (*lāzim*) is obtained from it). [This is] because nothing is understood of the named without it. And because the implicative consequence (*lāzim*) occurs without any temporal interruption between it and the named *implicative condition* (*malzūm*)[33].

س هل هذه الدلالاتُ لفظيّةٌ أم عقليّةٌ؟

---

٣١ هذا عند المناطقة بخلافه عند البيانيين والأصوليين فلا يشترط عندهم وجوده حيث قالوا: دلالة الالتزام: ما يفهم منه معنى خارج عن المسمى، أي: سواء كان الفهم للزوم بينها في ذهن كل واحد، أو عند العالم بالوضع، أو في خارج ولم يكن بينهما لزوم أصلًا لكن القرائن استلزمته.

32 Al-Fādānī: This is according to the logicians, as opposed to the rhetoricians and the scholars of principles of jurisprudence, who do not require such a condition since they said [that] *implicative signification* (*dalālat al-iltizām*) is what conveys a meaning external to the named referent, i.e. whether the understanding comes from an *implicative condition* (*luzūm*) between them in the mind of every individual, or in the mind of one knowledgeable of linguistic convention, or even externally without any inherent connection between them, but where the context necessitates it.

33 When A implies B, B is *what is implied* (*lāzim*, the *implicative consequence*) and A is *what implies it* (*malzūm, the implicative condition*). In such a relationship, A cannot exist unaccompanied by B, though B can exist unaccompanied by A. In the example of "human" implying "knowledge": "human" cannot exist unaccompanied by "knowledge," though "knowledge" can exist unaccompanied by "human."

ج   جميعُهــا لفظيّـةٌ قطعًا في دلالـةِ المطابقةِ، وعنـدَ الأكثرينَ[34] في غيرِها.

Q   Are these significations verbal or rational?

A   All of them are verbal, with certainty, for correspondence signification (*dalālat al-muṭābaqah*) and, according to the majority,[35] for the others.

س   إلى كَمْ تنقسمُ نسبةُ اللفظِ إلى مدلولِه؟

ج   تنقسمُ إلى خمسـةِ أقسامٍ: تَواطُؤٌ، وتَخالُفٌ، واشـتِراكٌ، وتَرادُفٌ، وتَشكيكٌ.

Q   The relationship between the utterance and what it signifies divides into how many divisions?

A   It has five divisions:
   1.   equipollent (*tawāṭu'*),
   2.   dissimilar (*takhāluf*),
   3.   homonymy (*ishtirāk*),
   4.   synonymy (*tarāduf*), and
   5.   non-uniform (*tashīk*).

س   ما هو التواطؤ؟

ج   هو أن يكونَ اللفظُ والمعنى مُتَّحِدَينِ، كَ «الإنسانِ» بالنسـبةِ إلى أفرادِ مدلولِه؛ فإنّه متّحدُ المعنى في كلٍّ مِنها.

Q   What is *equipollent* (*tawāṭu'*)?

A   It is the utterance and meaning being identical. Such as "human"

---

٣٤   وقيل: إن الدلالتين الأخيرتين عقليتان؛ لتوقفهما على انتقال الذهن من المعنى الموضوع له إلى جزئه أو لازمه.

35   Al-Fādānī: It has been said that the last two types of signification are rational, because they depend on the mind's transition from the designated meaning to its part or its implicative consequence.

in relation to members of what it signifies since its meaning is identical in all of them.

س   ما هو التخالفُ؟

ج   هو أن لا يكونَ اللفظُ والمعنى متّحدَينِ، كـ «الإنسانِ» و «الفرسِ»؛ فإنّ أحدَهما لا يَصدُقُ على ما يصدقُ عليه الآخَرُ .

Q   What is *dissimilar* (*al-takhāluf*)?
A   It is the utterance and the meaning not being identical. Such as "human" and "horse" since one is not true for what the other is.

س   ما هو الإشتراكُ؟

ج   هو أن يكونَ اللفظُ متّحدًا والمعنى مُتكثّرًا، كـ «العينِ»؛ فإنّ لفظَها واحـدٌ، ومعنـاه متكثّـرٌ، كـ «الذهبِ» و «الفضّـةِ » و «الباصرةِ» و «الجاسـوسِ»، وقد يُسمّى «اشتراكًا لفظيًّا» للاحترازِ عن الإشتراكِ المعنويِّ، وهو أن يتّحدَ اللفظُ والمعنى معًا لكن معناه صادقٌ على أفرادٍ كثيرينَ، كـ «الإنسانِ» و «العينِ» باعتبارِ صدقِه على «عينِ زيدٍ» و «[عينِ] بكرٍ» غيرِهما مِن أفرادِ الإنسانِ مثلًا.

Q   What is *homonymy* (*al-ishtirāk*)?
A   It is the utterance being identical while having multiple meanings. Such as "*ayn*" since its utterance is singular and its meanings are numerous, such as like "gold," "silver," "eye," ["substance,"] and "spy."
   It can also be called *verbal commonality* (*ishtirāk lafẓī*) to separate it from *semantic commonality* (*ishtirāk ma'nawī*), which is the utterance and meaning both being identical but applying to numerous members. Such as "human" and "*ayn*" with respect

to them applying to "Zayd's entity" and "Bakr['s entity]"[36] and other members of human—for example.

س   ما هو الترادفُ^(٣٧)؟

ج   هـو أن يكـونَ اللفظُ متكثِّـرًا والمعنـى متّحـدًا، كـ «الإنسـانِ» و «البشيرِ»، وكـ «الأسدِ» و «الليثِ»، وكـ «المطرِ» و «الغيثِ»؛ فإنّ اللفـظَ فـي كلِّ مِن الأمثلةِ الثلاثةِ متكثِّـرٌ والمعنى واحدٌ، وهو في الأوّلِ الحيـوانُ الناطقُ، وفي الثاني الحيوانُ المفترسُ، وفي الثالثِ القطرُ النازلُ مِن السماءِ.

Q   What is *synonymy* (*al-tarāduf*)?[38]

A   It is multiple utterances having an identical meaning. Such as "*al-insān*" and "*al-bashīr*," "*al-asad*" and "*al-layth*," and "*al-maṭar*" and "*al-ghayth*"[39] since each of the three examples have multiple utterances having a single meaning. In the first, it is the rational animal [i.e. human]; in the second, the predatory animal [i.e. lion]; and in the third, the drops that descend from the sky [i.e. rain].

س   ما هو التشكيكُ^(٤٠)؟

ج   هـو أن يكـونَ اللفـظُ والمعنـى متّحدَينِ ولكن معنـاه يتفاوتُ في

---

36   In this example, *'ayn* could refer to entity, substance, or eye. The Malay translation renders it as "zat" meaning "substance."

٣٧   ترى أن الترادف يقابل التخالف، كما أن التواطؤ يقابل الاشتراك.

38   Al-Fādānī: It is seen that *synonymy* (*tarāduf*) is the opposite of *antonymy* (*takhāluf*), just as *conceptual synonymy* (*tawāṭu'*) is the opposite of *homonymy* (*ishtirāk*).

39   English examples: "block" and "cube."

٤٠   سمي بذلك؛ لتردده بين التواطىء والاشتراك اللفظي بسبب توافق أفراده في أصل المعنى وباتحاد اللفظ وتكثر المعنى باعتبار الزيادة على أصل المعنى.

أفرادِهِ، إمّا بالشدّةِ، كـ «البياضِ»؛ فإنّ معناه في «الثلجِ» أشدُّ مِنه
في «العاجِ»، وكـ «الخضرةِ» في النباتِ؛ فإنّها في بعضِه أقوى مِن
الآخَـرِ، وإمّـا بالتقدُّمِ، كـ «الوجودِ»؛ فإنّ معناه في «الواجبِ» قبلَه
في «الممكنِ».

Q   What is *non-uniform* (*al-tashīk*, non-equipollent)?[41]
A   It is the utterance and meaning being identical but the meaning
    having gradations in its members, either
    1.   in intensity, such as "whiteness" since its meaning in "snow"
         is more intense than its meaning in "ivory," and such as
         "greenness" in plants since it is stronger in some than in
         others; or
    2.   in precedence, such as "existence" since its meaning in
         "necessary [existence]" comes before "possible [exist-
         ence]."

س   إلى كَمْ يَنقسِمُ التخالفُ؟
ج   يَنقسِمُ إلى أربعةِ أقسامٍ: مُساواةٌ، ومُباينةٌ، وعُمومٌ وخُصوصٌ مُطلقٌ،
    وعمومٌ وخصوصٌ وجهيٌّ.

Q   *Dissimilar* (*takhāluf*) divides into how many divisions?
A   It divides into four divisions:
    1.   equivalent (*musāwāh*),
    2.   separate (*mubāyanah*),
    3.   absolute universality and particularity (*'umūm wa khuṣūṣ
         muṭlaq*), and
    4.   overlapping universality and particularity (*'umūm wa
         khuṣūṣ wajhī*).

---

41   Al-Fādānī: It was named as such due to its oscillation between *conceptual
     synonymy* (*tawāṭu'*) and *verbal homonymy* (*ishtirāk*), because its instances
     agree on the core meaning while sharing the same word, and the meaning
     multiplies based on the addition to the core meaning.

س   ما هو المساواةُ؟

ج   هــو أن يَصــدُقَ^(٤٢) كلُّ واحـدٍ مِـن اللفظَيـنِ على كلِّ مـا يَصدُقُ عليـه الآخَـرُ، ويصـحُّ حمـلُ أحدِهما على الآخَرِ، كـ «إنسانٍ» و «ضاحكٍ»؛ فإنَّ كلَّ مـا يَصـدُقُ عليه «إنسانٌ» يَصـدُقُ عليه «ضاحـكٌ»^(٤٣) ويصـحُّ لـه عليه، فيُقالُ: «خالدٌ إنسانٌ» و «خالدٌ ضاحكٌ»، ويُسمَّى أيضًا «تَساويًّا».

Q   What is *equivalent* (*musāwāh*)?

A   It is that each of the utterances is true[44] for everything the other is true for and it is valid to predicate one upon the other. Such as "human" and "laughing" since everything that "human" is true for, "laughing" is true for; and is it is valid [to predicate it] upon it. So it is said, "Khalid is a human" and "Khalid is laughing."[45]

It is also called *equivalence* (*tasāwī*).

---

٤٢   الصدق هنا في أقسام التخالف من قبيل الصدق في المفردات بمعنى «الحمل»، بخلافه في القضايا فبمعنى «التحقق»، ثم المراد بالحمل هنا: حمل المواطأة -وهي: حمل هو هو- دون حمل الاشتقاق -وهو حمل المبتدأ بواسطة حمل المشتق، كحمل الضرب في «زيد ضارب» فإن إفادة قيامه به بواسطة حمل الضارب عليه-.

٤٣   ومن قبيل المساواة الرجم وزنا المحصن؛ لأن كل مرجوم زان محصن، وكل زان محصن مرجوم.

44   Al-Fādānī: Truth here, in the divisions of antonymy (*takhāluf*), falls under the category of truth in terms of individual terms, meaning *predication*, as opposed to its use in propositions, where it means *correspondence to reality*. The intended meaning of predication here is *univocal predication* (*ḥaml al-muwāṭa'ah*), which is the predication of the thing itself, not *derived predication* (*ḥaml al-ishtiqāq*), which is the predication of the subject through the predication of the derivative, as in the predication of "striking" in "Zayd is a striker," where its implication of the action being attributed to him is through the predication of "striker" upon him.

45   Al-Fādānī: An example of *equivalence* (*musāwāh*) is stoning and fornication perpetrated by a *muḥṣan* (one with the capacity to remain chaste), because every person who is stoned is a *muḥṣan* fornicator, and every *muḥṣan* fornicator is stoned.

س   ما هو المباينةُ؟

ج   هو أن لا يَصدُقَ واحدٌ مِنهُما على شيءٍ مِمّا يَصدُقُ عليه الآخَرُ، كـ «إنسانٍ» و «فرسٍ»(٤٦)، ويُسمّى أيضًا «تباينًا».

Q   What is *separate (mubāyanah)*?

A   It is that neither of them is true for what the other is true for. Such as "human" and "horse."[47]
It is also called *separatingly.*

س   ما هو العمومُ والخصوصُ المطلقُ؟

ج   هو أن يَصدُقَ واحدٌ مِن اللفظَين على كلِّ ما يَصدُقُ عليه الآخَرُ مِن غيرِ عكسٍ، كـ «إنسانٍ» و «حيوانٍ»(٤٨).

Q   What is *absolute universality and particularity (ʿumūm wa khuṣūṣ muṭlaq)*?

A   It is that one of the utterances is true for all that the other is true for, but not the opposite. Such as "human" and "animal."[49]

س   ما هو العمومُ والخصوصُ الوجهيُّ؟

ج   هو أن يَصدُقَ كلُّ واحدٍ مِن اللفظَين على بعضٍ ما يَصدُقُ عليه الآخَرُ، كـ «حيوانٍ» و «أبيضَ»(٥٠).

---

٤٦   ومن قبيل المباينة الإسلام والجزية.

47   Al-Fādānī: An example of *separate (mubāyanah)* is Islam and the *jizyah* [contract], as they are mutually exclusive categories.

٤٨   ومن قبيل العموم والخصوص المطلق: الغسل والإنزال؛ لأن كل منزل مغتسل وليس كل مغتسل منزلا؛ لأن المغتسل قد يكون غير منزل واغتساله للنظافة.

49   Al-Fādānī: Among the instances of *absolute generality and specificity* are bathing (*ghusl*) and sexual impurification (*inzāl*); because all with sexual impurification are bathers, but not bathers are with sexual impurification. This is because a bather might not be with sexual impurification, and the bath could be for cleanliness.

٥٠   ومن قبيل العموم والخصوص الوجهي: حل النكاح مع ملك اليمين؛ لأن بعض ما يحل نكاحه

Q   What is *overlapping universality and particularity ('umūm wa khuṣūṣ wajhī)*?

A   It is that each of the utterances is true for some of what the other is true for. Such as "animal" and "white."[51]

مملوك باليمين وبعضه بالعقد الصحيح وبعض المملوك باليمين يحل نكاحه وبعضه لا يحل.

51   Al-Fādānī: Among the instances of *overlapping universality and particularity* (*'umūm wa khuṣūṣ wajhī*) are lawfulness of intercourse and slavery; because some of what is lawful for intercourse is [through] slavery, while some is through a valid [marriage] contract. Additionally, some slaves are lawful for intercourse, while others are not.

3

THE PRINCIPLES OF

CONCEPTUALISATIONS

مبادئُ التصوُّراتِ: الكلّيّاتُ الخمسُ. المَقولاتُ العشرُ.

<table>
<tr><td>

3.1 THE FIVE [PREDICABLE] UNIVERSALS

</td><td dir="rtl">

الكلّيّاتُ الخمسُ

</td></tr>
</table>

س إلى كَمْ يَنقسمُ الكلّيُّ؟

ج يَنقسمُ إلى قسمَينِ: كلّيٌّ ذاتيٌّ، وكلّيٌّ عَرَضيٌّ.

Q Universals (*kullī*)[52] divide into how many divisions?
A They divide into two divisions:
1. essential universals (*kullī dhātī*) and
2. accidental universals (*kullī 'araḍī*).

س ما هو الكلّيُّ الذاتيُّ؟

ج هو ما كانَ داخلًا في ماهيّةٍ، أو ما لا يمكنُ فهمُ الحقيقةِ بدونه.

Q What is an *essential universal* (*kullī dhātī*)?

---

52 i.e. universal simple operational utterances.

A   It is what is intrinsic to a quiddity (*māhiyyah*) or what the true nature (*haqīqah*) cannot be understand without.

س   ما هو الكلّيُّ العرضيُّ؟

ج   هو ما كانَ خارجًا عن الماهيّةِ، أو ما يمكنُ فهمُ الحقيقةِ بدونِه.

Q   What is an *accidental universal* (*kullī ʿaradī*)?

A   It is what is extrinsic to the quiddity (*māhiyyah*) or what the true nature can be understood without.

س   إلى كَم يَنقسمُ الكلّيُّ الذاتيُّ؟

ج   يَنقسمُ إلى ثلاثةِ أقسامٍ: جنسٌ، ونَوعٌ، وفَصلٌ.

Q   Essential universals (*kullī dhātī*) divide into how many divisions?

A   They divide into three divisions
1. genus (*jins*),
3. species (*nawʿ*), and
3. differntia (*faṣl*).

س   إلى كَم يَنقسمُ الكلّيُّ العرضيُّ؟

ج   يَنقسمُ إلى قسمَينِ: عـرضٌ خـاصٌّ، وعـرضٌ عـامٌّ. فالكلّيّـاتُ خمسٌ^(٥٣).

Q   Accidental universals (*kullī ʿaradī*) divide into how many divisions?

---

٥٣ اعلم أن الألفاظ التي يستعملونها في محاوراتهم ستة: «منها: الكليات الخمس»، والسادس الشخص، ثم هذه الستة: ثلاثة منها تدل على الأعيان التي هي الموضوعات وهي الشخص والنوع والجنس»، وثلاثة منها دالة على الصفات وهي «الفصل، والعرض الخاص، والعرض العام».

A They divide into two divisions:
1. specific accident (*'araḍ khāṣṣ*) and
2. general accident (*'araḍ 'āmm*).
Thus, the universals (*kulliyyāt*) are five.[54]

س   ما هو الجنسُ؟

ج   هو كلِّيٌّ مقولٌ على كثيرينَ مختلفينَ بالحقيقةِ في جوابِ «ما هو»، وبعبارةٍ أخصرُ: هو صفةُ جماعةٍ مختلفةِ الصوَّرِ يَعُمُّها معنىً واحدٌ، كـ «الحيوانِ» بالنسبةِ إلى «الإنسانِ» وغيرِه مِن أنواعِ الحيواناتِ؛ فأنواعُ الحيواناتِ مِن «إنسانٍ» و «بقرٍ» و «فيلٍ» و «سمكٍ» كثرةٌ مختلفةُ الصوَّرِ يَعُمُّها معنىً واحدٌ يُعبَّرُ عنه بـ «حيوانٍ»، وهذا هو الجنسُ.

Q   What is a *genus* (*jins*)?
A   It is a universal said for many members differing in their true nature in response to "What is it?" More concisely expressed: It is an attribute of a group differing [in their] forms [yet] comprising a single meaning. Such as "animal" in relation to "human" and other species of animals since the species of animals—including "human," "bovine," "elephantine," and "fish"—are multitudes with differing forms having a single meaning common to them referred to as the *genus* (*jins*).

س   إلى كَمْ يَنقسمُ الجنسُ؟

ج   يَنقسمُ إلى قسمَينِ: جنسٌ قريبٌ، وجنسٌ بعيدٌ.

---

54 Al-Fādānī: Know that the terms they use in their discussions are six. They include the five universals; the sixth is the *personal* (*shakhṣ*). These six are divided as follows: three of them indicate substances, which are the individual, species, and genus; and three indicate attributes, which are the differentia, the specific accident, and the general accident.

Q   The genus (*jins*) divides into how many divisions?
A   It divides into two divisions:
1.   proximate genus (*jins qarīb*) and
2.   remote genus (*jins baʿīd*).

س   ما هو الجنسُ القريبُ؟

ج   هو ما لا جنسَ تحتَه، كـ «حيوانٍ» بالنسبةِ لِـ «إنسانٍ».

Q   What is a *proximate genus* (*jins qarib*)?
A   It is what has no genus below it. Such as "animal" in relation to "human."

س   ما هو الجنسُ البعيدُ؟

ج   هـو مـا كانَ تحتَه جنـسٌ أو أجناسٌ فيكونُ بعيدًا بمرتبةٍ كـ «نامٍ» بالنسـبةِ لِـ «إنسانٍ»، أو بعيدًا بمرتبتَينِ كـ «جسمٍ مطلقٍ» بالنسبةِ له، أو بثلاثِ مراتبَ كـ «جوهرٍ» بالنسبةِ له.

Q   What is a *remote genus* (*jins baʿīd*)?
A   It is what has one or more genera below it.
    It is remote by:
    — one level, such as "growing" in relation to "human";
    — two levels, such as "absolute body" in relation to it [i.e. "human"]); or
    — three levels, such as "primary substance (*jawhar*)" in relation to it [i.e. "human"].

س   ما هو النوعُ؟

ج   هـو كلّـيٌّ مقولٌ علـى كثيرينَ مختلفِينَ بالعـددِ دونَ الحقيقةِ في جـوابِ «ما هـو»، وبعبارةٍ أخصرَ: هو صفةُ جماعةٍ مُتَّفِقةٍ بالصورة

وَيَعُمُّهــا معنـىً واحدٌ، كـ «إنسانٍ» بالنسـبةِ إلى أفـرادِه؛ فإنّ هذه الأفرادَ كثرةٌ متّفقةُ الصّورِ يَعُمُّها معنـىً واحدٌ، يُعَبَّرُ عنه بـ «إنسانٍ»، وهذا هو النوعُ.

Q   What is a *species* (nawʻ)?

A   It is a universal said of many members differing in their number but not their true nature in response to "What is it?" More concisely expressed: It is an attribute of a group with matching forms having a single meaning common to them all. Such as "human" in relation to its members since these members are a multitude with a matching form having a single meaning common to them expressed as "human"—and this is the species.

س   ما هو الفصلُ(٥٥)؟

ج   هــو كلّــيٌّ مقولٌ على كثيرينَ مختلفيــنَ بالعــددِ دونَ الحقيقةِ في جــوابِ «أيُّ نــوع هــو في ذاتِـه»، وبعبارةٍ أوضحَ: هــو الصفةُ التي لا يُتصــوَّرُ الموصوفُ إلّا بهــا ومتى بطَلت بطَلَ الموصوفُ، كـ «ناطــقٍ»(٥٦) بالنسبةِ إلى «الإنسانِ» فإنّ النطـقَ الفكريَّ صفةٌ لا يُتصوَّرُ الـ «إنسانُ» إلّا به.

Q   What is a *differentia* (faṣl)?[57]

A   It is a universal said of many members differing in their number but not their essential realty, in response to "What species is it in its true nature?" More concisely expressed: It is an attribute that the thing described cannot be conceived of except with it

---

٥٥   إنما سمي «فصلًا»؛ لأنه يفصل الجنس فيجعله نوعًا، وبه يحد النوع.

٥٦   ومن أمثلة الفصل: «حرارة النار، ورطوبة الماء، ويبوسة الحجر، ونمو النبات، والحس والحركة في الحيوان، والتلون في الحبر».

57   Al-Fādānī: It is called *differentia* (faṣl) because it separates the genus, making it a species, and through it, the species is defined.

and, when it is nullified, so, too, is the described thing. Such as "rational"[58] with respect to "human" since rationality is an attribute that "human" is inconceivable without it.

س إلى كَمْ يَنقسمُ الفصلُ؟

ج يَنقسمُ إلى قسمَينِ: فصلٌ قريبٌ، وفصلٌ بعيدٌ.

Q   The differentia (*faṣl*) divides into how many divisions?
A   It divides into two divisions:
   1.   proximate differentia (*faṣl qarīb*) and
   2.   remote differentia (*faṣl baʿīd*).

س ما هو الفصلُ القريبُ؟

ج هو ما يُميِّزُ الشيءَ عن جنسِه القريبِ، كَ «ناطقٍ» لِـ «إنسانٍ».

Q   What is a *proximate differentia* (*faṣl qarīb*)?
A   It is what distinguishes a thing from its proximate genus (*jins qarīb*). Such as "rational being" for "human."

س ما هو الفصلُ البعيدُ؟

ج هو ما يُميِّزُ الشيءَ عن جنسِه البعيدِ كَ «حسَّاسٍ» لِـ «إنسانٍ».

Q   What is a *distant differentia* (*faṣl baʿīd*),?
A   It is what distinguishes a thing from its remote genus (*jins baʿīd*). Such as "sensitive" for "human."

س ما هو العرضُ الخاصُّ؟

---

58   Al-Fādānī: Examples of *differentia* (*faṣl*) include: the heat of fire, the moisture of water, the dryness of stone, the growth of plants, sensation and movement in animals, and colouration in ink.

ج هــو كلّــيٌّ مقولٌ علــى كثيرينَ مختلفيــنَ بالعــددِ دونَ الحقيقةِ في جــوابِ «أيُّ عرضٍ هو»، ويُســمّى أيضًا «خاصّةٌ» كـ «الضاحكِ» بالنسبةِ إلى «الإنسانِ».

Q   What is a *specific accident* (ʿaraḍ khāṣṣ)?

A   It is a universal said of many members differing in their number but not their true nature, in response to "What accident is it?" It is also called *property* (khāṣṣah). Such as "laughing" in relation to "human."

س ها هو العرضُ العامُّ؟

ج هو كلّيٌّ مقولٌ على كثيرينَ مختلفينَ بالحقيقةِ إلّا أنّه لا يُقالُ في الجوابِ أصلًا، كـ «ماشٍ» بالنسبةِ إلى «الإنسانِ».

Q   What is a *general accident* (ʿaraḍ ʿāmm)?

A   It is a universal said of many members differing in their true nature except that it is not said in direct response to a question. Such as "walking" in relation to "human."

س إلى كَمْ يَنقسمُ العرضُ مطلقًا؟

ج يَنقسمُ إلى قسمَينِ: عرضٌ لازمٌ، وعرضٌ مُفارقٌ.

Q   Accidents (ʿaraḍ), in absolute terms, divide into how many divisions?

A   They divide into two divisions:
1.   inseparable accident (ʿaraḍ lāzim) and
2.   separable accident (ʿaraḍ mufāriq).

س ما هو العرضُ اللازمُ[59]؟

---

[59]   وقد يعرف خصوص «العرض الخاص اللازم»: بأنه صفة تكون في جميع أفراد النوع كل حين في جميع العمر، ويسمون أيضًا: «خاص الخاص». ومن أمثلته: «البكاء للإنسان، والصهيل للخيل، والنهيق للحمار».

ج   هو ما امتنعَ انفكاكُه عن معروضِه، كـ «ضاحكٍ بالقوّةٍ» بالنسـبةِ لِـ «إنسانٍ»، وكـ «متحرّكٍ ومتنفّسٍ بالقوّةٍ» بالنسبةِ لِـ «حيوانٍ».

Q   What is an *inseparable accident* (*'araḍ lāzim*)?[60]

A   It is what is impossible to separate from its *accident-recipient* (*ma'rūd*). Such as "potential to laugh" in relation to "human." And such as "potential to move and breathe" in relation to "animal."

س   ما هو العرضُ المفارقُ[61]؟

ج   هو مـا لـم يمتنع انفكاكُه عن معروضِـه، كـ «ضاحكٍ بالفعلِ» بالنسبةِ لِـ «إنسانٍ».

Q   What is a *separable accident* (*'araḍ mufāriq*)?[62]

A   It is what is not impossible to separate from its accident-recipient (*ma'rūd*). Such as "actually laughing" in relation to "human."

س   ما هي مراتبُ الأجناسِ المتسلسلةِ؟

ج   مراتبُها ثلاثَةٌ: جنسٌ عالٍ، وجنسٌ سافلٌ، وجنسٌ متوسّطٌ.

---

60   Al-Fādānī: The specific *inseparable specific accident* (*'araḍ khāṣṣ lāzim*) may be defined as an attribute that is found in all individuals of the species at all times throughout their lifespan. It is also referred to as *proprium* (*khāṣṣ al-khāṣṣ*). Examples of this include: crying for humans, neighing for horses, and braying for donkeys.

٦١   وقد يعرف خصوص «العرض الخاص المفارق»: بأنه صفة تكون في بعض أفراد النوع، أو في جميع أفراده ولكن في وقت دون وقت، فالأول كالكتابة والنجارة والحدادة، والثاني كالشيب في الإنسان فإنه يكون في آخر العمر.

62   Al-Fādānī: The specific *separable specific accident* (*'araḍ khāṣṣ mufāriq*) is defined as an attribute that exists in some individuals of a species, or in all individuals but only at certain times. The first case includes attributes like writing, carpentry, and blacksmithing. The second case includes attributes like grey hair in humans, which appears later in life.

Q   What are the sequential ranks of the genera?
A   Their ranks are three:
1.   high genus (*jins ʿālī*),
2.   low genus (*jins sāfil*), and
3.   intermediate genus (*jins mutawassiṭ*).

س   ما هو الجنسُ العالِيُّ؟

ج   هــو مــا لا جنسَ فوقَه وتحتَه أجناسٌ، وهو أعمُّ الأجناسِ، ويُـسـمَّى
«جنسَ الأجناسِ» أيضًا، كـ «الجوهرِ» و «الكَمِّ».

Q   What is the *high genus* (*jins ʿālī*)?
A   It is what has no genus above it while having genera below it. It
is the most general genus. It is also called *summum genus* (*jins
al-ajnās*). Such as "primary substance" (*jawhar*) and "quantity"
(*kamm*).

س   ما هو الجنسُ السافِلُ؟

ج   هو ما كانت فوقَه أجناسٌ وتحتَه أنواعٌ، أو هو أخصُّ الأجناسِ، كـ
«الحيوانِ».

Q   What is the *low genus* (*jins sāfil*)?
A   It is what has genera above it while having species (*nawʿ*) below
it, or it is the most specific genus. Such as "animal."

س   ما هو الجنسُ المتوسِّطُ؟

ج   هــو مــا كــانَ فوقَـه جنسٌ وتحتَه كذلـك، أو هو مــا كــانَ أعمَّ مِن
الجنسِ السافلِ وأخصُّ مِن الجنسِ العالِيِّ، كـ «الجسمِ النامي» و
«مطلقِ الجسمِ».

Q   What is an *intermediate genus* (*jins mutawassiṭ*)?

A   It is what has a genus above it while having the same below it,
     or it is what is more general than the lowest genus and more
     specific than the highest genus. Such as "growing body" and
     "absolute body."

3.2 THE TEN CATEGORIES   المَقولاتُ العشرُ

س   كَمْ أقسامُ الجنسِ العاليِّ؟

ج   أقسـامُه عشرةٌ^(٦٣)، وتُسـمّى «المَقولاتِ العَشرَ»^(٦٤)، وهي: جوهرٌ،
     وكَـمٌّ، وكيـفَ، وإضافةٌ، وأينَ، ومتى، ومِلـكٌ، ووَضعٌ، وأن يَفعَلَ،
     وأن يَنفعِلَ، والتسعةُ الأخيرةُ أعراضٌ.

Q   How many divisions is the high genus (*jins ʿālī*)?
A   It has ten categories.[65] They are called the *Ten Categories* (*maqūlāt
     ʿashr*).[66] They are:

     1.   primary substance (*jawhar*),

---

٦٣   وليس يشذ عنها شيء في هذا الكون، فلا شيء في دارِك، أو في حقلك، أو في السماء، أو
     الكواكب إلا وهو داخل في هذه الأقسام العشرة.

٦٤   قد جمع بعضهم هذه المقولات العشر في قوله: قمر غزير الحسن ألطف مصره * قد قام
     يكشف غمتي لما انثنى

     فأشار إلى الجوهر بقوله «قمر»، وإلى الكم بقوله «غزير» أي: كثير، وإلى الكيف بقوله
     «الحسن»، وإلى الإضافة بقوله «ألطف»، وإلى الأين بقوله «مصره»، وإلى الوضع بقوله
     «قام»، وإلى أن يفعل بقوله «يكشف»، وإلى الملك بقوله «غمتي»، وإلى المتن بقوله
     «لما»، وإلى أن ينفعل بقوله «انثنى».

65   Al-Fādānī: Nothing in this universe escapes from these categories; there is
     nothing in your house, in your field, in the sky, or among the planets except
     that it falls within these ten categories.

66   Al-Fādānī: Some have compiled the ten categories in the following verse:
     A moon, abundant in beauty, with the finest of lands, *
     He stood, uncovering my sorrow when he turned away."
     He alluded to *substance* with the word "moon"; to *quantity* with "abundant,"
     i.e. much; to *quality* with "beauty"; to *relation* with "finest"; to *place* with
     "land"; to *position* with "stood"; to *action* with "uncovering"; to *possession*
     with "my sorrow"; to *time* with "when"; and to *passion* with "turned away."

2. quantity (*kamm*),
3. quality (*kayf*),
4. relation (*iḍāfah*),
5. place (*ayn*),
6. time (*matā*),
7. possession (*milk*),
8. position (*waḍʿ*),
9. action (*an yafʿal*), and
10. passion (*an yanfaʿil*).

The last nine are *accidents* (*aʿrāḍ*, pl. of *ʿaraḍ*).

س   ما هو الجوهرُ؟

ج   هـو القائـمُ بِنفسِـه والقابـلُ للأعـراضِ المتضـادّةِ، كـ «ذواتِنا» و «الحُقولِ» و «الأمتِعَةِ» و «المَباني».

Q   What is a *primary substance* (*jawhar*)?

A   It is what is self-subsistent and receptive to contradictory accidents. Such as "our essences," "fields," "baggage," and "buildings."

س   ما هو العرضُ؟

ج   هو القائمُ بالجوهرِ ويكونُ الجوهرُ مَوصوفًا به.

Q   What is an *accident* (*ʿaraḍ*)?

A   It is what subsists in a primary substance (*jawhar*) and the primary substance is characterised by it.

س   ما هو الكمُّ؟

ج   هو المِقدارُ، وشأنُه أن يَقبَلَ القِسمةَ لذاتِه.

Q   What is a *quantity* (*kamm*)?

A It is a measure. Its nature is that its disposition is being receptive to being divided by its very essence (*li-dhātihi*).

س إلى كَمْ يَنقسمُ الكمُّ؟

ج يَنقسمُ إلى قسمَينِ:

١. كمٌّ مُنفَصِلٍ، كـ «خمسةٍ» مِن «خمسةِ قُروشٍ»؛ فإنّها منفصلةٌ عن معدوداتِها القُروشِ،

٢. وكمٌّ متّصلٍ، كـ «سطحِ المنزلِ»؛ فإنّه متّصلٌ بالمنزلِ.

Q Quantity (*kamm*) divides into how many divisions?
A It divides into two divisions.
   1. External quantity (*kamm munfaṣil*). Such as "five" in "five cents" [lit. *qurṣūsh*] since it is detached from the cents it quantifies.
   2. Internal quantity (*kamm muttaṣil*). Such as ["roof" in] "the roof of the house" since it is attached to the house.

س ما هو الكيفُ؟

ج هو عرضٌ شأنُه أن لا يَقبَلَ القسمةَ واللاقسمةَ لذاتِه، وأن لا يتوقَّفَ تصوُّرُه على تصوُّرِ غيرِه، كـ «الألوانِ»(٦٧).

Q What is a *quality* (*kayf*)?
A It is an accident whose nature is that it is not receptive to division or non-division by its very essence (*li-dhātihi*), and its conceptualisation does not depend upon the conceptualisation of something else. Such as "colours."[68]

---

٦٧ وكالحلاوة والمرارة ورائحة زكية ومنتنة ونعومة وخشونة ونور وظلمة وصوت قوي وضعيف.

68 Al-Fādānī: Like sweetness and bitterness, a pleasant and foul smell, softness and roughness, light and darkness, and a strong and weak sound.

س   ما هي الإضافةُ؟

ج   هـي النسبَةُ العارضــةُ للجسـمِ بالقيـاسِ إلـى قسـمةٍ أُخـرى، كـ «الأُبـوّةِ»^(٦٩) العارضةِ للأبِ و «البُنـوّةِ» العارضةِ للابـنِ؛ فإنّ كلًّا مِنهما نسبةٌ تُعقَلُ بالقياسِ إلى نسبةٍ أُخرى.

Q   What is a *relation (iḍāfah)*?

A   It is a relation incidental to the body by analogy to another division. Such as "fatherhood"[70] is incidental to the father and "filiality" is incidental to the son since each of them is a relation reasoned via analogy to another relation.

س   ما هو الأينَ؟

ج   هو حصولُ الشيءِ في المكانِ^(٧١).

Q   What is a *place (al-ayn)*?

A   It is the thing occurring within a location.[72]

س   إلى كَمْ يَنقسمُ الأينَ؟

ج   يَنقسمُ إلى قسمَينِ: أينَ حقيقيٌّ، وأينَ غيرُ حقيقيٍّ.

---

٦٩   وما أشبههيا من الأسماء التي تقع بين اثنين مشتركين في معنى، وذلك المعنى ليس موجودًا في هاتين الذاتين، وإنما هو في نفس المتفكر كالأخوة والزوجية، وكون الشخص جارًّا أو صديقًا أو شريكًا وأصغر أو أكبر وأجمل وأغنى.

70   Al-Fādānī: And similar to these are the terms that exist between two entities sharing a common meaning, though that meaning is not inherently present in either of the two entities themselves, but rather exists in the mind of the one contemplating them—such as brotherhood and marriage; a person being a neighbour or friend or partner; or being younger or older; or being more beautiful, or wealthier.

٧١   مثل: فوق وتحت.

72   Al-Fādānī: Like above and below.

Q   Place (*ayn*) divides into how many divisions?
A   It divides into two divisions:
1.   literal place (*'ayn ḥaqīqī*) and
2.   non-literal place (*'ayn ghayr ḥaqīqī*).

س   ما هو الأَينَ الحقيقيُّ؟

ج   هو حصولُ الشيءٍ في مكانِه المُختَصِّ به.

Q   What is a *literal place* (*'ayn ḥaqīqī*)?
A   It is the thing occurring in a place exclusive to it.

س   ما هو الأَينَ الغيرُ الحقيقيُّ؟

ج   هو حصولُ الشيءٍ في مكانِه الذي لا يَختَصُّ به، ككونِ خالد في
مدرسةٍ أو بلدٍ كذا.

Q   What is a *non-literal place* (*'ayn ghayr ḥaqīqī*)?
A   It is the thing occurring in a place that is not exclusive to it.
Such as Khalid being in such-and-such school or land.

س   ما هو المتى؟

ج   هو حصولُ الشيءٍ في الزمانِ^(٧٣).

Q   What is a *time* (*matā*)?
A   It is the thing occurring within time.[74]

س   إلى كَمْ تنقسمُ المتى؟

ج   يَنقسمُ كالأَينِ إلى قسمَينِ: متى حقيقيٌّ، ومتى غيرُ حقيقيٍّ.

---

٧٣   كساعة ويوم وليلة وشهر وسنة.

74   Al-Fādānī: Like hour, day, night, month, and year.

Q   Time (*matā*) divides into how many divisions?
A   It, like place, divides into two divisions:
1.   literal time (*matā ḥaqīqī*) and
2.   non-literal time (*matā ghayr ḥaqīqī*).

س   ما هو المتى الحقيقيُّ؟

ج   هو حصولُ الشيءٍ في الزمانِ الذي ينطبقُ عليه، ككونِ الكُسوفِ في وقتٍ كذا.

Q   What is a *literal time* (*matā ḥaqīqī*)?
A   It is the thing occurring in the time to which it applies. Such as the eclipse being in such-and-such time.

س   ما هو المتى غيرُ الحقيقيٍّ؟

ج   هو حصولُ الشيءٍ في الزمانِ الـذي لا ينطبـقُ عليـه، ككونِ الكُسوفِ في يومٍ كذا أو شهرٍ كذا.

Q   What is a *non-literal time* (*matā ghayr ḥaqīqī*)?
A   It is the thing occurring in the time to which it does not correspond to it. Such as the eclipse being in such-and-such day or month.

س   ما هو المِلكُ؟

ج   هو هيئةٌ حاصلةٌ للشـيءٍ بسـببِ مـا يحيطُ بـه أو ببعضِه، وينتقلُ بانتقالِه كالهيئةِ^(٧٥) الحاصلةِ بالتعمُّمِ والتقمُّصِ والتسلُّحِ.

Q   What is a *possession* (*al-milk*)?
A   It is a manner resulting for the thing because of what encompasses it or a part of it and which moves through its movement. Such as the manner[76] resulting from donning a turban, wearing a shirt, and being armed.

---

٧٥   وككون زيد يملك دارًا وعقارًا وله حلم وخلق وعلم.

76   Al-Fādānī: Like Zayd owning a house and property, and having patience, character, and knowledge.

س إلى كَمْ يَنقسمُ المُحيطُ المُنتَقِلُ؟

ج يَنقسمُ إلى قسمَينِ: طبيعيٌّ كـ «جلدِ الحيوانِ»، وغيرُ طبيعيٍّ سواءٌ أحاطَ بالكلِّ، كـ «الثوبِ»، أو بالبعضِ، كـ «الخاتَمِ».

Q The *moving environment* (*muḥīṭ muntaqil*) divides into how many divisions?

A It divides into two divisions:

1. natural (*ṭabīʿī*), such as an animal's skin; and
2. unnatural (*ghayr ṭabīʿī*), whether it encompassed the whole, such as a garment, or the part, such as a ring.

س ما هو الوضعُ؟

ج هو هيئةٌ حاصلةٌ للشيءِ بسببِ نسبتَينِ؛ هما نسبةُ[77] بعضِ أجزائه إلى بعضٍ، ونسبةُ أجزائِه[78] إلى الأمورِ الخارجـةِ عنه، كـ «هيئةِ الإنسانِ في القيامِ»؛ فإنّه يُعتبَرُ فيه نسبةُ أجزاءِ الجسمِ بعضِها إلى بعضٍ، ونسبةُ تلك الأجزاءِ إلى أمورٍ خارجةٍ عنها[79]، كمثلِ «كَونِ رأسِه مِن فوقٍ ورجلَيه مِن أسفلَ[80]».

Q What is a *position* (*waḍʿ*)?

A It is a manner resulting for a thing because of two relations:

1 the relation[81] of some of its parts to others and
2 the relation of its parts[82] to things external to it.

Such as a human's manner during standing, since the relation of parts of the body to one another is considered therein, and

---

٧٧ بالقرب والبعد والمحاذاة وغيرها.

٧٨ بأن تختلف بها الأجزاء في الموازاة والانحراف والقرب والبعد بالقياس إلى جهات العالم.

٧٩ ولا تكفي النسبة الأولى فقط في الوضع وإلا لزم أن يكون الانعكاس قيامًا.

٨٠ وكهيئة الإنسان في استلقائه وقعوده وانبطاحه ونومه وهيئة الحديقة والحقل والمساكن فإن لها هيهات خاصة.

81 Al-Fādānī: Like proximity, distance, parallel, and other such terms.

82 Al-Fādānī: Whereby the parts differ in alignment, deviation, proximity, and distance in relation to the directions of the world.

[so is] the relation of those parts to things external to it.[83] And such as, for example, his head being above and his feet below.[84]

س   ما هو «أنْ يَفْعَلَ»؟

ج   هو كَوْنُ[٨٥] الشيءِ مؤثِّرًا في غيرِه، كـ «القاطِعِ»[٨٦] ما دامَ قاطعًا .

Q   What is an *action* (*an yaf'al*)?

A   It is a thing being[87] an influence over something else. Such as "the interruptor"[88] so long as it interrupts.

س   ما هو «أنْ يَنفَعِلَ»؟

ج   هـو كَوْنُ[٨٩] الشــيءِ متأثِّـرًا مِـن غيرِه، كـ «المنقطِعِ»[٩٠] ما دامَ منقطعًا .

Q   What is *passion* (*an yanfa'il*)?

A   It is a thing being[91] influenced by something else. Such as "the interrupted"[92] so long as it is interrupted.

---

83   Al-Fādānī: The first relation alone is not sufficient for determining position; otherwise, reflection would be considered standing.

84   Al-Fādānī: Like the arragement of a human being when lying down, sitting, sprawling, or sleeping, and the arrangement of a garden, field, or dwellings, as each has its own specific forms.

٨٥   فهو غير مبدأ الفعل لبقائه بعد.

٨٦   وكالنار والثلج والصانع والمعلم.

87   Al-Fādānī: Thus, it is not the principle of action, as it remains afterward.

88   Al-Fādānī: Like fire and ice, the craftsman and the teacher.

٨٩   فهو غير أثر الفعل لبقائه بعد فإن يفعل وأن ينفعل إنما يقال على التأثير والتأثر ما داما فإذا انقضيا يقال لهما الفعل والانفعال.

٩٠   وكالكرسي والباب والبناء والمفتاح والزراعة وما أشبه ذلك من كل مصنوع أو قابل للأثر كالمحرق بالنار والغريق والمأكول والمضروب والمشروب.

91   Al-Fādānī: Thus, it is distinct from the effect of the action, as it remains afterward. For action and passion are terms used for the process of influence and being influenced while they are ongoing. Once they have ended, they are referred to as the act and the reaction.

92   Al-Fādānī: Like the chair, the door, the building, the key, agriculture, and similar things, whether crafted or subject to an effect, such as what is burned by fire, drowned, eaten, struck, or drunk.

4

THE PURPOSES OF CONCEPTUALISATIONS

مقاصدُ التصوُّراتِ

المُعَرِّفاتُ

4.1 DEFINIENTIA

س   ما هو المُعَرِّفُ؟

ج   هو ما يُقالُ على الشيءٍ لإفادةِ تصوُّرِه.

Q   What is a *definiens* (*mu'arrif*)?
A   It is what is said about a thing to communicate its conceptualisation.

س   إلى كَمْ يَنقسمُ المعرِّفُ؟

ج   يَنقسمُ إلى ثلاثةِ أقسامٍ: حدٌّ، ورُسومٌ، ولفظيٌّ.

Q   The definiens (*mu'arrif*) divides into how many divisions?
A   It divides into three divisions:
   1.   limit-definition (*ḥadd*),
   2.   sketch-definition (*rusūm*), and
   3.   verbal (*lafẓī*).

س   ما هو الحدُّ؟

ج   هو ما يكونُ بجميعِ الذاتيّاتِ أو بعضِها، ويُسـمّى «مُعَرِّفًا حقيقيًّا» أيضًا.

Q   What is a *limit-definition* (*ḥadd*)?

A   It is what is through all or some of the essentials. It is also called a *proper definiens* (*muʿarrif ḥaqīqī*).

س إلى كَمْ يَنقسمُ الحدُّ؟

ج يَنقسمُ إلى قسمَينِ: حدٌّ تامٌّ، وحدٌّ ناقصٌ.

Q   The limit-definition (*ḥadd*) divides into how many divisions?

A   It divides into two divisions:

1.   complete limit-definition (*ḥadd tāmm*) and
2.   incomplete limit-definition (*ḥadd nāqiṣ*).

س ما هو: الحدُّ التامُّ؟

ج هو ما يكونُ بجميعِ (٩٣) الذاتيّاتِ، -أَعني: ما يكونُ بالجنسِ والفصلِ القريبَينِ- كتعريفِ «الإنسانِ» (٩٤) بأَنّه «حيوانٌ ناطقٌ».

Q   What is a *complete limit-definition* (*ḥadd tāmm*)?

A   It is what is through all[95] the essentials, meaning: the proximate genus and [proximate] differentia (*jins qarīb*, *faṣl qarīb*). Such as defining "human"[96] as "rational animal."

س ما هو الحدُّ الناقصُ؟

ج هو ما يكونُ ببعضِ الذاتيّاتِ، -أَعني بالجنسِ البعيدِ (٩٧) والفصلِ

---

٩٣ ولهذا لا يجوز أن يكون للشيء حدان تامان فيستحيل أن يكون النوع الواحد له فصلان على البدل بخلاف الرسم واللفظيّ فلا يمتنع تعددهما لجواز تعدد الخواص والألفاظ المترادفة.

٩٤ وتعريف الخمر بأنه: «شراب مسكر معتصر من العنب».

95   Al-Fādīnī: For this reason, it is not possible for a thing to have two complete limit-definitions. It is impossible for a single species to have two differentiae that alternate. However, this does not apply to the sketch-definition (*rasm*) and the verbal definition (*lafẓī*), as it is not impossible for them to be multiple, given the possibility of multiple properties and synonymous terms.

96   Al-Fādānī: And defining wine as "an intoxicating drink pressed from grapes."

٩٧ مثل الجنس البعيد فصله على التحقيق، كتعريف الإنسان: بأنه «حساس ناطق».

القريبِ- كتعريفِ الإنسانِ بأنّه «جسمٌ ناطقٌ»، أو بالفصلِ القريبِ
وحدَهُ^(٩٨)، كتعريفِ «الإنسانِ» بأنّه «ناطقٌ».

Q What is an *incomplete limit-definition (ḥadd nāqiṣ)*?

A It is what is through some of the essentials, meaning:
   — the far genus[99] and the proximate differentia (*jins baʿīd, faṣl qarīb*), such as defining "human" as being "rational body"), or
   — the proximate differentia (*faṣl qarīb*) alone,[100] such as defining "human" as "rational."

س ما هو الرسمُ؟

ج هـو ما يكونُ ببعضِ الذاتيّاتِ مـع العرضيّاتِ أو بالعرضيّاتِ فقط،
يُسمّى «مُعَرِّفًا رسميًّا» أيضًا.

Q What is a *sketch-definition (rasm)*?

A It is what is through some of the essentials with [its] accidents or just the accidents. It is also called a *depictive definiens (muʿarif rasmī)*.

س إلى كَمْ يَنقسمُ الرسمُ؟

ج يَنقسمُ إلى قسمَينِ أيضًا: رسمٌ تامٌّ، ورسمٌ ناقصٌ.

Q The sketch-definition (*rasm*) divides into how many divisions?

A It also divides into two divisions:
   1. complete sketch-definition (*rasm tāmm*) and
   2. incomplete sketch-definition (*rasm nāqiṣ*).

---

٩٨ بناء على جواز التعريف بالمفرد، والأصحّ عدم جوازه، فلا يجوز التعريف إلا بمتعدد.

99 Al-Fādānī: Like the far genus and its true differentia, as in the definition of a human being as "a sentient, rational being."

100 Al-Fādānī: This is based on the possibility of defining with a single term, but the soundest view is that it is not possible, so a definition must consist of multiple elements.

س   ما هو الرسمُ التامُّ؟

ج   هــو مــا يكــونُ بالجنـسٍ القريـبِ والخاصَّـةِ اللازمـةِ لـه، كتعريفِ
«الإنسانِ» بأنَّه «حيوانٌ ضاحكٌ».

Q   What is a *complete sketch-definition* (*rasm tāmm*)?
A   It is what is through the proximate genus (*jins qarīb*) and its
inseparable specific accident (*khāṣṣah lāzimah lahu*). Such as
defining "human" as "laughing animal."

س   ما هو الرسمُ الناقصُ؟

ج   هــو مــا يكــونُ بالخاصَّـةِ فقــط، كتعريـفِ «الإنسانِ»[101] بأنَّه
«ضاحكٌ».

Q   What is an *incomplete sketch-definition* (*rasm nāqiṣ*)?
A   It is what is through just the inseparable specific accident
(*khāṣṣah*). Such as defining "human"[102] as "laughing."

س   ما شرطُ تَمامِ الحَدِّ والرسمِ؟

ج   شــرطُه تقديـمُ الجنـسِ، فلــو أخَّرَ الجنـسُ عن الفصـلِ كانَ حدًّا
ناقصًا، أو أخَّرَه عن الخاصَّةِ كانَ رسمًا ناقصًا.

Q   What is the condition for the limit-definition and sketch-definition being complete?
A   Its condition is the genus coming first. Thus:
— if the genus (*jins*) comes after the differentia (*faṣl*), it is an
incomplete limit-definition (*ḥadd nāqiṣ*); or
— if it comes after the inseparable specific accident (*khāṣṣah*),
it is an incomplete sketch-definition (*rasm nāqiṣ*).

---

١٠١   وكتعريف الخمر: بأنه مائع يقذف بالزبد.

102   Al-Fādānī: Like the definition of wine as "a liquid that produces froth."

س   ما هو المُعَرِّفُ اللفظيُّ؟

ج   هـو لفـظٌ مبدلٌ عن لفظٍ آخَرَ، وكانَ أشـهرَ مِنه مرادفًا له، كتعريفِ
«القمحِ» بـ «البُرِّ» وتعريفِ «العُقارِ» بـ «الخمرِ».

Q   What is a *verbal definiens* (*muʿarrif lafẓī*)?

A   It is one utterance substituting another utterance while [the
former] is better known and synonymous to [the later]. Such
as defining "*al-qamḥ*" with "*al-burr*" (wheat), or "*al-ʿuqār*"
with "*al-khamr*" (wine).

س   ما هي شُروطُ المُعَرِّفِ؟

ج   يُشترَطُ له خمسةُ أُمورٍ:
أحدُها أن يكونَ مُطَّرِدًا، أي: مانعًا مِن دُخولِ شـيءٍ مِن أفرادِ غير
المُعَرَّفِ،
وثانيًا أن يكونَ مُنعَكِسًا، أي: جامعًا لأفرادِ المُعَرَّفِ،
وثالثًا أن يكونَ ظاهرًا[103]،
ورابعُها أن يُجتنَبَ فيه الألفاظُ الغريبةُ المشتركةُ المَجازيّةُ[104]،
وخامسُها -وهو[105] خاصٌّ بالحدِّ- أن لا تُذكَرَ «أو»[106].

Q   What are the conditions of the definiens (*muʿarrif*)?

A   Five things are conditions for it:
The first is being restrictive (*muṭṭarid*), i.e. preventing (*māniʿ*)
the entrance of anything that is not a member of what is being
defined.

---

١٠٣ فلا يعرف الشيء بالأخفى، كقولهم في تعريف النار: بأنه «جسم كالنفس» ولا يعرف بما
يتوقف تعقله على تعقل غيره للزوم الدور.
١٠٤ لئلا يلزم إلى بيانها فتطول المسافة.
١٠٥ لأن النوع الواحد يستحيل أن يكون له فصلان عن البدل بخلاف الخاصتين.
١٠٦ نعم بجوز ذكر «أو» في الحد بجعلها للتقسيم والتنويع كا في تعريفهم النظر: بأنه الفكر المؤدي
إلى علم أو ظن.

The second is being consistent (*mun'akis*), i.e. including (*jāmi'*) the members of what is being defined.

The third is being apparent (*ẓāhir*).[107]

The fourth is avoiding utterances that are strange (*gharībah*), homonymous (*mushtarakah*), and figurative (*majāziyyah*).[108]

The fifth (which is[109] specific to the limit-definition) is not mentioning "or" (*aw*).[110]

---

107 Al-Fādānī: Thus, something cannot be defined by something even more obscure, as in their definition of fire as "a body like the soul." Nor can it be defined by something whose intellection depends on the intellection of something else, as this would result in circular reasoning.

108 Al-Fādānī: So as to avoid the necessity of further explanation, which would unnecessarily extend the discussion.

109 Al-Fādānī: Because it is impossible for a single species to have two alternating differentiae, unlike two distinct properties, which can coexist without contradiction.

110 Al-Fādānī: Indeed, it is permissible to mention "or" in a definition by using it for division and classification, as in their definition of *reasoning* (*naẓar*) as "thought that leads to knowledge or conjecture."

5

THE PRINCIPLES OF ASSENTS:

PROPOSITIONS, CONTRADICTORIES &

CONVERSION

مبادئُ التصديقاتِ: القضيّةُ - نَقيضُها - عَكسُها

<table>
<tr><td>5.1 PROPOSITIONS</td><td align="right">(القضايا)</td></tr>
</table>

س   ما هي القضيّةُ؟

ج   هي القولُ الذي يَصِحُّ أن يُقالَ لقائِلِه إنّه صادقٌ أو كاذبٌ.

Q   What is a *proposition* (*qaḍiyyah*)?

A   It is a statement [for] which it is valid to say to its utterer that he is truthful (*ṣādiq*) or lying (*kādhib*).

س   إلى كَمْ يَنقسمُ القضيّةُ؟

ج   تنقسمُ إلى قسمَينِ: حَمليّةٌ، وشَرطيّةٌ.

Q   Propositions (*qaḍiyyah*) divide into how many divisions?

A   They divide into two divisions:
1.   categorical (*ḥamliyyah*) and
2.   conditional (*sharṭiyyah*).

55

س   ما هي القضيّةُ الحمليّةُ(١١١)؟

ج   هي التي يكونُ طرفاها مفردَينِ، نحوُ: «خالدٌ حاضرٌ».

Q   What is a *categorical proposition* (*qaḍiyyah ḥamliyyah*, lit. *predicative proposition*)?[112]

A   It is one whose two parts are simple utterances (*lafẓ mustaʿmal mufrad*). Such as "Khalid is present."

س   ما هي أجزاءُ الحمليّةِ؟

ج   أجزاؤُها ثلاثةٌ:

الأوّلُ: يُسمّى «مَوضوعًا»(١١٣)، وهو الطَّـرَفُ الأوّلُ مِـن طرفَيها، ويُسمّى أيضًا «مَحكومًا عليه»،

والثاني: يُسمّى «مَحمولًا»(١١٤)، وهو الطرفُ الثاني مِنهُما، يُسمّى أيضًا «مَحكومًا به»،

والجـزءُ الثالـثُ: هـو النسبـةُ الواقعـةُ بينَها، وقد يـدلُّ عليها بلفظٍ يُسمّى «رابِطةً»(١١٥).

---

١١١ وقد تسمى «مقدمة» إذا وقعت صغرى أو كبرى قياس، و «نتيجة» إذا جاءت أثر قياس، و «دعوى» إذا لم تكن أثر قياس ولم يكن هناك خصم، و «مطلوبا» إن كان هناك خصم، إذن فهذه أسماء مختلفة التراكيب، والمسمى شيء واحد.

112 Al-Fādānī: It may be called a *premise* (*muqaddimah*) when it appears as the minor or major term in a syllogism, a *conclusion* (*natījah*) when it is the result of a syllogism, a *claim* (*daʿwā*) when it is not the result of a syllogism and there is no opponent, and a *subject of inquiry* (*maṭlūb*) when there is an opponent. Thus, these are different names with varying structures, but the underlying concept is one and the same.

١١٣ لأنه وضع للحكم عليه بشيء.

١١٤ لحمله على شيء.

١١٥ من هنا علم أن لفظ الرابطة لا يلزم ذكره، بل يجوز حذفه؛ لدلالة الحال عليه؛ أو لعدم الاحتياج إليه نحو قولك: «قام خالد».

Q   What are the components of a categorical proposition (*qaḍiyyah ḥamliyyah*)?

A   Its has three components:

The first is called the *subject* (*mawḍūʿ*).[116] It is the first of the two parts. It is also called the *recipient of the assertion* (*maḥkūm ʿalayhi*).

The second is called the *predicate* (*maḥmūl*).[117] It is the second part of the two [parts]. It is also called the *assertion received* (*maḥkūm bihi*).

The third is the *relationship* (*nisbah*) existing between the two. It can also be indicated through an utterance named a *copula* (*rābiṭah*).[118]

س   ما هي الرابطةُ؟

ج   هي لفظٌ دالٌّ على النسبةِ الواقعةِ بينَ طرفَي الحمليّةِ.

Q   What is a *copula* (*rābiṭah*)?

A   It is an utterance indicating the relationship existing between the two parts of the categorical proposition (*qaḍiyyah ḥamliyyah*).

س   إلى كَمْ تنقسمُ الرابطةُ؟

ج   تنقسمُ إلى قسمَينِ: رابطةٌ زمانيّةٌ بأَن تكونَ فعلًا ناسخًا للابتداءِ، كلفظِ «كانَ» و «وُجِدَ»، ورابطةٌ غيرُ زمانيّةٍ بأن كانت اسمًّا، كلفظِ «هو».

---

116   Al-Fādānī: Because it is designated for making an assertion about it in relation to something else.

117   Al-Fādānī: For predicating it of something.

118   Al-Fādānī: From this, it is understood that the *copula* (*rābiṭa*) does not necessarily need to be mentioned; rather, it can be omitted due to the context indicating it or because it is not needed, as in your saying: "Khālid stood."

Q   The copula (*rābiṭah*) divides into how many divisions?

A   They divide into two divisions.

1.   A *temporal copula* (*rābiṭah zamāniyyah*) by being a verb abrogating instantiation (*nāsikh li-l-ibtidā'*). Such as the utterances "was" (*kān*) and "was existent" (*wujida*).

2.   A *non-temporal copula* (*rābiṭah ghayr zamāniyyah*) by it being a noun. Such as the utterance "him" (*huwa*).

س   لِمَ سُمِّيَت «حمليّةً»؟

ج   لِما فيها مِن الحَملِ، وهو الحكمُ بثُبوتِ شيءٍ لشيءٍ أو نفيُه عنه.

Q   Why is it [the categorical proposition, the *ḥamliyyah*, which is literally a predicative proposition] called "predicative"?

A   Because of the predication (*ḥaml*) it contains, which is the assertion that something is affirmed to something else or negated from it.

س   ما هي القضيّةُ الشرطيّةُ؟

ج   هي التي لا يكونُ طرفاها مفردَينِ بأن كانتا قضيّتَينِ حمليّتَينِ على نهجٍ مخصوصٍ(١١٩)، أو التي يُحكَمُ فيها على التعليقِ بشرطٍ.

Q   What is a *conditional proposition* (*qaḍiyyah sharṭiyyah*)?

A   It is [either]

1.   one whose two parts are not simple operational utterances (*lafẓ musta'mal mufrad*) by them being two categorical propositions (*qaḍiyyatayn ḥamaliyyatayn*) in the form of exclusive propositions (*makhṣūṣ*),[120] or

---

١١٩   فإذا قلت: «إن كانت الشمس طالعة، فالنهار موجود» فهذه القضية الواحدة فيها قضيتان حمليتان، فقولك «الشمس طالعة» قضية حملية، وقولك «النهار موجودا» قضية حملية أخرى، وبإدخالك لفظة «إن» صارتا قضية شرطية متصلة، شرط فيها وجود المقدم لوجود التالي بكلمة شرط.

120   Al-Fādānī: When you say, "If the sun is rising, then the day exists," this single proposition contains two categorical propositions. Your statement "the sun

2. it is the one whose assertion is contingent upon a condition (*shart*).

س ما هي أجزاءُ الشرطيّةُ؟

ج لهـا جزآنِ فقط، الأوّلُ: يُسـمّى ‹‹مُقَدَّمًـا››^(١٢١)؛ وهو الطرفُ الأوّلُ مِـن طرفَيها. والثاني: يُسـمّى ‹‹تاليًا››^(١٢٢)؛ وهو الطرفُ الآخَرُ، ولا رابطةَ بينَهـما.

Q What are the components of a conditional proposition (*qaḍiyyah sharṭiyyah*)?

A It has just two components.
The first is called an *antecedent* (*muqaddam*),[123] which is the first of the two parts.
The second is called *consequent* (*tālī*)[124], which is the second part.
There is no copula (*rābiṭah*) between the two.

س لِمَ سُمِّيَت ‹‹شرطيّةً››؟

ج لوجودِ أداةِ الشرطِ فيها.

Q Why is it called "conditional" (*sharṭiyyah*)?
A Because of the existence of a conditional operand (*adāt al-sharṭ*) within it.

---

is rising" is a categorical proposition, and your statement "the day exists" is another categorical proposition. By introducing the word "if," these two become a conjunctive conditional proposition, where the existence of the antecedent is a condition for the existence of the consequent, by virtue of the conditional term.

١٢١ لتقدمه لفظًا أو حكمًا.
١٢٢ لتلوه الأوّل، أي: تبعيته.

123 Al-Fādānī: Due to its precedence, either in wording or in assertion.
124 Al-Fādānī: Since it follows the first, meaning it is subordinate to it.

س إلى كَمْ تنقسمُ الحمليّةُ باعتبارِ النسبةِ؟

ج تنقسمُ إلى قسمَينِ: مُوجَبةٍ، وسالِبةٍ.

Q Categorical propositions (*ḥamliyyah*), with respect to the relation (*nisbah*), divide into how many divisions?

A They divide into two divisions:
   1. affirmative (*mūjabah*) and
   2. negative (*sālibah*).

س ما هي الحمليّةُ الموجبةُ؟

ج هــي التـي يكــونُ الحكمُ فيها بثُبوتِ شيءٍ لشيءٍ، نحوُ: «كلُّ إنسانٍ حيوانٌ».

Q What is an *affirmative categorical proposition* (*qaḍiyyah ḥamliyyah mūjabah*)?

A It is one whose assertion therein is to affirm something to something [else]. Such as "Every human is an animal."

س ما هي الحمليّةُ السالبةُ؟

ج هي التي يكونُ الحكمُ فيها بنفيِ شيءٍ عن شيءٍ، نحوُ: «لا شيءَ مِن الإنسانِ بحجرٍ».

Q What is a *negative categorical proposition* (*qaḍiyyah ḥamliyyah sālibah*)?

A It is one whose assertion therein is to negate something from something [else], such as, "No human is a rock."

س إلى كَمْ تنقسمُ الحمليّةُ باعتبارِ المَوضوعِ؟

ج تنقســمُ إلى أربعةِ أقسامٍ: شَــخصيّةٍ، وجُزئيّةٍ، وكُلّيّةٍ، ومُهمَلةٍ، وزادَ بعضُهم قِسمًا خامسًا، هو الطبيعيّةِ(١٢٥).

———————

١٢٥ وقد تركها الأكثرون؛ لأنها ليست معتبرة في مسائل العلوم.

5.1 PROPOSITIONS

Q The categorical proposition (*qaḍiyyah ḥamliyyah*), with respect to the subject (*mawḍūʿ*), divides into how many divisions?

A It divides into four divisions:
1. singular (*shakhṣiyyah*),
2. particular (*juzʾiyyah*),
3. universal (*kulliyyah*), and
4. indeterminate (*muhmalah*).

Some added a fifth category:
5. natural (*ṭabīʿiyah*).[126]

س‏ ما هي الشخصيّةُ؟

ج‏ هـي التـي يكونُ المحكـومُ عليه فيها جزئيًّا مُعَيَّنًا، نحـوُ: «خالدٌ كاتبٌ»، وتُسمّى أيضًا «مَخصوصةً»(١٢٧).

Q What is a *personal categorical proposition* (*qaḍiyyah ḥamliyyah shakhṣiyyah*)?

A It is one where the thing asserted therein is a specified particular (*juzʾī muʿayyan*), such as "Khālid is a writer." It is also called an *exclusive categorical proposition* (*qaḍiyyah ḥamliyyah makhṣūṣah*).[128]

س‏ ما هي الجزئيّةُ؟

ج‏ هي التي يكونُ المحكومُ عليه فيها جزئيًّا غير معيّنٍ، بذكرِ السـورِ الجزئـيِّ؛ وهـو «بعضٌ» و «واحدٌ» في الموجبةِ، و «ليسَ بعضُ» و «بعضُ ليسَ» في السالبةِ، نحوُ: «بعضُ الإنسانِ كاتبٌ».

---

126 Al-Fādānī: Most have omitted it because it is not considered relevant in the issues of the sciences.

١٢٧ إنما سميت «شخصية»؛ لتشخص؛ أو خصوص موضوعها، وهي في حكم الكلية، ولهذا اعتبرت في كبرى الشكل الأول، فيقال: «هذا خالد» و «خالد إنسان».

128 Al-Fādānī: It is called *personal* (*shakhṣiyyah*) due to its specificity or the particularity of its subject, yet it functions as a universal. For this reason, it is considered in the major premise of the first figure of syllogism, as in saying: "This is Khālid" and "Khaalid is a human."

Q What is a *particular categorical proposition (qaḍiyyah ḥamliyyah juz'iyyah)*?

A It is one where the thing asserted therein is a non-specific particular by mentioning a particular quantifier (*sūr juz'ī*), which is:
   — "some" (*ba'ḍ*) and "one" (*wāḥid*) in the affirmative, and
   — "it is not that some" (*laysa ba'ḍ*) and "some are not" (*ba'ḍ laysa*) in the negative.
   Such as "Some humans are writers."

س ما هي الكلّيّةُ؟

ج هي التي يكونُ المحكومُ عليه فيها كلّيًّا بذكرِ السورِ الكلّيِّ؛ وهو «كلٌّ» و «أل» الاستغراقيّةِ أو العهديّةِ في الموجبةِ و «لا شـــيءَ» و «لا واحدَ» في السالبةِ، نحوُ: «كلُّ إنسانٍ حيوانٌ».

Q What is a *universal categorical proposition (qaḍiyyah ḥamliyyah kulliyyah)*?

A It is one where the thing asserted therein is a universal by mentioning a universal quantifier (*sūr kullī*), which is:
   — "all" (*kull*) and "the" (*al-*) for universal inclusivity (*istighrāqiyyah*) or what is already mentioned (*'ahadiyyah*) in the affirmative, and
   — "nothing" and "no one" in the negative.
   Such as "Every human is an animal."

وتُسمّى هي والجزئيّةُ «مَحصورةً» و «مُسَوَّرَةً» أيضًا.

It [the universal] and the particular are called *quantified* (*maḥṣūrah*, lit. circumscribed) and *walled off* (*musawwarah*).

س   ما هي المهملةُ^(۱۲۹)؟

ج   هي التي يكونُ المحكومُ عليه فيها غيرُ مُبَيَّنٍ كمّيّةٍ أفرادِه، ولكنّها صالحةٌ لأن تَصدُقَ كلّيّةً أو جزئيّةً، نحوُ: «الإنسانُ كاتبٌ».

Q   What is an *indeterminate categorical proposition* (*qaḍiyyah ḥam-liyyah muhmalah*, lit. *neglected*)?[130]

A   It is one where the thing asserted therein has an unspecified quantity of members, though it is valid to be true as a universal or a particular. Such as "The human is a writer."

س   ما هي الطبيعيّةُ؟

ج   هـي التـي لم يُبَيَّن فيها كمّيّةُ الأفرادِ، ولم تَصلُح لأن تصدُقَ كلّيّةً أو جزئيّةً، نحوُ: «الحيوانُ جنسٌ»، و«الإنسانُ نوعٌ».

Q   What is a *natural categorical proposition* (*qaḍiyyah ḥamliyyah ṭabīʿiyyah*)?

A   It is one wherein the quantity of members (*kammiyat al-afrād*) is not clarified, and it is not valid to be true as a universal or a particular. Such as "The animal is a genus" and "The human is a species."

س   إلى كَمْ تنقسمُ الشرطيّةُ؟

ج   تنقسمُ إلى قسمَينِ: متَّصِلَةٍ، ومُنفَصِلَةٍ.

Q   The *conditional proposition* (*qaḍiyyah sharṭiyyah*) divides into how many divisions?

---

۱۲۹   وهذه في قوة الجزئية على الصحيح؛ لاحتمالها الكل، والبعض، وهو المتيقن فتحمل عليها.

130   Al-Fādānī: This is equivalent to a *particular proposition* (*qaḍiyyah juzʾiyyah*) according to the correct view, because it can potentially refer to the whole or to some, and since it [i.e. the latter] is certain, it is interpreted as such.

A   It is divided into two divisions:
1.   conjunctive (*muttaṣilah*) and
2.   disjunctive (*munfaṣilah*).

س   ما هي الشرطيّةُ المتّصلةُ؟

ج   هـي التـي يُحكَمُ فيها بصدقِ قضيّـةٍ^(١٣١) أو لا صدقِها على تقديرِ صدقٍ أُخرى^(١٣٢).

Q   What is a *conjunctive conditional proposition* (*qaḍiyyah sharṭiyyah muttaṣilah*)?
A   It is one where the truth and non-truth of a proposition[133] is asserted based on the truthfulness of another [proposition].[134]

س   إلى كَمْ تنقسمُ الشرطيّةُ المتّصلةُ؟

ج   تنقسمُ إلى قسمَينِ: لُزوميّةٍ، واتِّفاقيّةٍ.

Q   The *conjunctive conditional proposition* (*qaḍiyyah sharṭiyyah muttaṣilah*) divides into how many divisions?
A   It is divided into two divisions:
1.   implicative (*luzūmiyyah*) and
2.   coincidental (*ittifāqiyyah*).

س   ما هي اللُزوميّةُ؟

ج   هي التي يُحكَمُ فيها بصدقِ قضيّةٍ أو لا صدقِها على تقديرِ صدقٍ أُخرى لعلاقةٍ.

---

١٣١ هي التالي.
١٣٢ هي المقدّم.

133 Al-Fādānī: Which is the consequent.
134 Al-Fādānī: Which is the antecedent.

Q   What is an *implicative conjunctive conditional proposition* (*qaḍi-yyah sharṭiyyah muttaṣilah luzūmiyyah*)?

A   It is one where the truth and non-truth of a proposition is asserted based on the truthfulness of another [proposition] due to a connection.

س   إلى كَمْ تنقسمُ اللُزوميّةُ مِن حيثُ علاقتُها؟

ج   تنقسمُ إلى قسمَينِ: قطعيّةٍ، وظنّيّةٍ.

Q   The *implicative conjunctive conditional proposition* (*qaḍiyyah sharṭiyyah muttaṣilah luzūmiyyah*), with respect to its connection (*'alāqah*), divides into how many divisions?

A   It is divided into two divisions:
1.   certain (*yaqīniyyah*) and
2.   presumptive (*ẓanniyyah*).

س   ما هي اللُزوميّةُ القطعيّةُ؟

ج   هي اللُزوميّةُ التي كانت العلاقةُ فيها توجِبُ ذلك الحكمَ، كالعِلّيّةِ⁽¹³⁵⁾، والتضايُفِ⁽¹³⁶⁾، نحوُ: «إن كانت الشمسُ طالعةً فالنهارُ مَوجودٌ»؛ إذ المقدَّمُ عِلّةٌ للتالي.

Q   What is a *certain implicative conjunctive conditional proposition* (*qaḍiyyah sharṭiyyah muttaṣilah luzūmiyyah qaṭ'iyyah*)?

A   It is an implicative proposition whose connection (*'alāqah*) therein brings about that assertion. Such as the *causative* (*'il-*

---

١٣٥   أي: ككون المقدم علة للتالي نحو المثال المذكور، وكذا المعلولية، أي: كون المقدم معلولًا للتالي نحو «إن كان النهار موجودًا فالشمس طالعة»، وكذا كون المقدم والتالي معلولي علة واحدة نحو: « إن كان النهار موجودًا فالعالم مضيء».

١٣٦   نحو: «إن كان زيد أبًا لخالد فخالد ابنه».

iyyah)[137] and *interdependent* (*taḍāyuf*).[138] Such as "If the sun is risen, then daytime is present" since the antecedent (*muqaddam*) is the cause of the consequent (*tālī*).

س   ما هي اللُزوميّةُ الظنّيّةُ؟

ج   هـي اللُزوميّـةُ التي كانت العلاقةُ فيهـا تُرَجِّحُ ذلك الحكمَ، نحوُ: «إن كانَ الغَيمُ مَوجودًا فالمَطَر يَعقِبُهُ».

Q   What is a *presumptively implicative conjunctive conditional proposition* (*qaḍiyyah sharṭiyyah muttaṣilah luzūmiyyah ẓanniyyah*)?

A   It is an implicative proposition whose connection therein prepoderates that assertion. Such as "If clouds are present, then rain will follow them."

س   ما هي الاتّفاقيّةُ؟

ج   هي التي يُحكَمُ فيها بصدقِ قضيّةٍ أو لا صدقِها على تقديرِ صدقِ أُخـرى، لا لعلاقةٍ، بل لِمُجَرَّدِ الصُّحبَةِ والازدِواجِ، نحوُ: «إن كانَ الإنسـانُ ناطقًا فالحِمارُ ناهِقٌ»، إذ لا علاقةَ بينَ ناطقيّةِ الإنسانِ وناهقيّةِ الحمارِ حتّى يَستلزِمَ، أو يُرَجِّحَ ترتُّبَ الثانيّةِ على الأولى بل تَوافَقا على الصدقِ هُنا.

Q   What is a *coincidental conjunctive conditional proposition* (*qaḍiyyah sharṭiyyah muttaṣilah ittifāqiyyah*)?

---

137   Al-Fādānī: That is, like the antecedent serving as a cause for the consequent, as in the previously mentioned example. And likewise *causality*, (*maʿlūliyyah*), meaning the antecedent is the effect of the consequent, as in "If the day exists, then the sun is rising." Additionally, both the antecedent and the consequent can be effects of the same cause, as in "If the day exists, then the world is illuminated."

138   Al-Fādānī: An example would be: "If Zayd is Khalid's father, then Khālid is his son."

A   It is one where the truth and non-truth of a proposition is asserted based on the truthfulness of another proposition—not because of a connection (ʿalāqah) but purely for accompanyment (ṣuḥbah) and being correlation (izdiwājiyyah). Such as "If humans are rational, then donkeys bray" since there is no connection between human rationality and donkeys braying such that it demands or preponderates the second being consequential to the first. Rather, their truth is coincidentally true.

س   ما هي الشرطيّةُ المنفصلةُ؟

ج   هي التي يُحكَمُ فيها بامتناعِ اجتماعِ قضيّتَينِ أو أكثرَ في الجُملةِ.

Q   What is a *disjunctive conditional proposition* (*qaḍiyyah sharṭiyyah munfaṣilah*)?

A   It is one where it is asserted therein to be impossible for two or more propositions to coincide in the sentence.

س   إلى كَمْ تنقسمُ المنفصلةُ؟

ج   تنقسمُ إلى ثلاثةِ أقسامٍ: حقيقيّةٍ، ومانعةِ جمعٍ، ومانعةِ خُلوٍّ.

Q   The disjunctive conditional proposition (*qaḍiyyah sharṭiyyah munfaṣilah*) divides into how many divisions?

A   It is divided into three divisions:
1.   proper (*ḥaqīqī*),
2.   anti-combinatorial (*māniʿat al-jamʿ*), and
3.   anti-exlusionary (*māniʿat al-khuluww*).

س   ما هي المنفصلةُ الحقيقيّةُ؟

ج   هي التي يُحكَمُ فيها بالتنافي بينَ طرفَيها صدقًا وكذبًا، أي: بأنّهما لا يجتمعانِ ولا يرتفعانِ. وتُسمّى أيضًا «مانعةَ الجمعِ والخُلوِّ

مَعًـا»، كقولِـك «العَـدَدُ إمّـا زوجٌ أو فـردٌ»؛ فيمتنعُ اجتمـاعُ الزوجِ والفردِ في عددٍ، ويمتنعُ خُلُوُّ العددِ عن كلٍّ مِنهما، وكقولِ النحاةِ: «الكلمةُ إمّا اسمٌ، وإمّا فعلٌ، وإمّا حرفٌ».

Q   What is a *proper disjunctive conditional proposition (qaḍiyyah sharṭiyyah munfaṣilah ḥaqīqiyyah)*?

A   It is one wherein it is asserted that the two parts are mutually inconsistent with respect to being true and false, i.e. they cannot both occur nor neither occur. It is also called *joint anti-combinatorial and anti-exclusionary (māni'at al-jam' wa-l-khuluww ma'an)*. Such as you saying, "A number is either even or odd" since it is impossible for even and odd to coincide in a number, and it is impossible for a number to be devoid of them both. And such as grammarians saying, "A word is either a noun, a verb, or a particle."

س   ما هي مانعةُ الجمعِ؟

ج   هي التي يُحكَمُ فيها بالتنافي بينَ طرفَيها صدقًا فقط؛ أي: بأنّهما لا يجتمعانِ، نحوُ: «هذا إمّا حيوانٌ وإمّا شـجرٌ»؛ فيمتنعُ اجتماعُ الحيوانِ والشجرِ، ويمكنُ الخُلُوُّ عنهما بأن يكونَ حائطًا أو مَعدِنًا.

Q   What is an *anti-combinatorial disjunctive conditional proposition (qaḍiyyah sharṭiyyah munfaṣilah māni'at al-jam')*?

A   It is one wherein it is asserted that the two parts are mutually inconsistent only with respect to being true, i.e. that they cannot coincide. Such as "This [thing] is either an animal or either a tree" since it is impossible for "animal" and "tree" to coincide, while it is possible to be devoid of them both by being a "wall" or "mineral."

س ما هي مانعةُ الخُلوِّ؟

ج هـي التـي يُحكَمُ فيها بالتنافي بينَ طرفَيها كذبًا فقط، أي: بأنّهما لا يرتفعـانِ، نحـوُ قولِـك: «هذا إمّا نام، وإمّا شـجرٌ» فهـذه تَمنَعُ الخُلـوَّ ولا تَمنَـعُ الجمعَ، ونحوُ: «زيدٌ إمّا أن يكونَ في الماءِ، وإمّا أن لا يَغـرِقَ»؛ فيمكـنُ اجتماعُهمـا، بأن يكونَ زيـدٌ في الماءِ ولا يَغرِقَ، ويمتنعُ خُلوُّ زيدٍ عنهما، بأن يكونَ في غير الماءِ ويَغرِقُ.

Q What is an *anti-exclusionary disjunctive conditional proposition* (*qaḍiyyah sharṭiyyah munfaṣilah māniʿat al-khuluww*)?

A It is one wherein it is asserted that two parts are mutually inconsistent only with respect to being false, i.e. that they cannot both be removed. Such as "This [thing] either grows or it is a tree" since this bars being free but not coinciding. And such as, "Zaid is either in the water or is not drowning" since it is possible for the two to coincide by Zaid being in the water and not drowning, while it is impossible for Zaid to be free of them both by being in something other than water while drowning.

التناقُضُ (١٤١)

5.2 CONTRADICTION[139]

س   ما هي التناقُضُ؟

ج   هـو اخـتلافُ قضيّتَينِ بالإيجـابِ والسـلبِ بحيـثُ إذا صَدَقَت إحداهُهما كَذِبَت الأُخرى بالضرورةِ.

Q   What is a *contradiction* (*tanāquḍ*)?

A   It is two propositions differing in affirmation (*ījāb*) and negation (*salb*) such that when one is true the other is false.

ش: ما شرطُ تَحَقُّقِ التناقضِ؟

ج   إذا كانـت القضيّـةُ شـخصيّةً أو مهملـةً فلا يَتحقَّقُ التناقضُ بينَ قضيّتَينِ مِنها إلّا بشرطِ تَساويهِما في الأُمورِ الثمانيّةِ المعبَّرِ عنها بـ «الوَحداتِ»، وهي: في المَوضوعِ، وفي المَحمولِ، وفي المكانِ، [وفي الزمامِ،] وفي الإضافةِ، وفي القوّةِ والفعلِ، وفي الكلِّ والجزءِ، وفي الشرطِ.

---

139   Al-Fādānī: Know that a proposition is like the sunlight, its *converse* (*ʿaks*) is like its shadow, and its *contradictory* (*naqīḍ*) is like the night. If it is not possible to establish a *demonstrative proof* (*burhān*) for a given proposition, we either prove the falsity of its contradictory, thereby making the proposition necessarily true, or we prove the truth of its converse, and thus the proposition becomes true as well.

140   Al-Fādānī: Know that a proposition is like the sunlight, its converse (*ʿaks*) is like its shadow, and its contradictory (*naqīḍ*) is like the night. If it is not possible to establish a demonstrative proof (*burhān*) for a given proposition, we either prove the falsity of its contradictory, thereby making the proposition necessarily true, or we prove the truth of its converse, and thus the proposition becomes true as well.

١٤١   اعلم أن القضية أشبه بنور الشمس، والعكس ظلها، والنقيض كالليل، فإذا لم يمكن إقامة البرهان على قضية ما أقمناه إما على بطلان نقيضها فتصدق هي ضرورة، أو على صدق عكسها فتصدق هي كذلك.

فالشـخصيّةُ، نحوُ: «خالـدٌ قائمٌ»، نَقيضُها: «خالـدٌ ليسَ بِقائمٍ» وبالعكسِ.

والمهملةُ، نحوُ: «الإنسانُ حيوانٌ»، نَقيضُها: «الإنسانُ ليسَ بحيوانٍ» وبالعكسِ.

وإذا كانت القضيّةُ جزئيّةً أو كلّيّةً فلا يَتحقّقُ التناقضُ بينَ قضيّتَينِ مِنها إلّا بشرطِ اخـتلافٍ في الكمّيّةِ[142] -أعني الكلّيّةَ والجزئيّةَ- زيادةً على اختلافِهما في الكيفِ -أعني الإيجابَ والسلبَ-، وفي ذلك أربعُ صُوَرٍ:

Q What are the conditions for contradiction (*tanāquḍ*) occurring?

A When the proposition is personal (*shakhṣiyyah*) or indeterminate (*muhmalah*), then contradiction does not occur between two propositions of their type except with the condition of them being equal in eight matters referred to as the *unities* (*waḥdāt*). They are the

1. subject (*mawḍū'*),
2. predicate (*maḥmūl*),
3. place (*makān*),
4. [time (*zamān*),]
5. relation (*iḍāfah*),
6. potentiality and actuality (*quwwat wa fi'l*),
7. whole and part (*kull wa juz'*), and
8. condition (*sharṭ*).

For the personal proposition (*qaḍiyyah shakhṣiyyah*), such as in "Khalid is standing," its contradictory is "Khalid is not

---

١٤٢ لأن الكلّيتين قد تكونان كاذبتين كقولنا: «كل إنسان كاتب» و «لا أحد من الإنسان بكاتب»، والجزئيتين قد تكونان صادقتين كقولك «بعض الإنسان كاتب» و «بعض الناس ليس بكاتب» فلا يكون صدق إحداهما وكذب الأخرى مطردًا، هذا وقد جعل بعضهم المهملة في قوة الجزئية وهو الصحيح كما قدمنا، فيكون نقيضها كلية مخالفة لها في الكيف، كما أن نقيض الجزئية كلية مخالفة لها في الكيف، وعليه فنحو «الإنسان حيوان» نقيضه «لا شيء من الإنسان بحيوان»، ونحو «بعض الإنسان ليس بحيوان» نقيضه وكل إنسان حيوان».

standing" and by conversion [i.e. "Some of those standing are Khālid"].

For the indeterminate (*al-muhmalah*), such as in "Humans are animals" its contradictory is "The human is not an animal" and by conversion [i.e. Some animals are humans."

When the proposition is particular (*juz'iyyah*) or universal (*kulliyyah*), contradiction (*tanāquḍ*) does not occur between two propositions of their type except with the condition of them differing in the quantity (*kamm*)[143]—meaning being universal and particular (*al-kulliyyah wa-l-juz'iyyah*)—in addition to them differing in the quality (*kayf*)—meaning being affirmative and negative (*al-ījāb wa-l-salb*).

There are four scenarios for this [as follows].

س   ما نَقيضُ الموجبةِ الكلّيّةِ؟

ج   نَقيضُها السـالبةُ الجزئيّةُ، نحوُ: «كلُّ إنسانٍ حيوانٌ» نَقيضُه «ليسَ بعضُ الإنسانِ بحيوانٍ».

Q   What is the contradictory of the affirmative universal (*naqīḍ* of the *mūjabah kulliyyah*)?

A   Its contradictory is the negative particular (*sālibah juz'iyyah*). Such as "Every human is an animal": its contradictory is "It is not that some people are animals."

---

143   Al-Fādānī: Because two universal propositions can both be false, as in the statements "Every human is a writer" and "No human is a writer"; and two particular propositions can both be true, as in "Some humans are writers" and "Some humans are not writers." Therefore, the truth of one and the falsity of the other is not a consistent rule. Some have considered *indeterminate propositions* (*muhmalah*) to be equivalent to *particular propositions* (*juz'iyyah*), which is the correct view, as we mentioned earlier. Based on this, the contradictory of a *universal proposition* (*kulliyyah*) is another universal proposition with the opposite *quality* (*kayf*), just as the contradictory of a particular proposition is a universal one with the opposite quality. Thus, a statement like "Humans are animals" is contradicted by "No human is an animal," and the statement "Some humans are not animals" is contradicted by "All humans are animals."

س   ما نَقيضُ الموجبةِ الجزئيّةِ؟

ج   نَقيضُها السالبةُ الكلّيّةُ، نحوُ: «بعضُ الإنسانِ حجرٌ» نقيضُه «لا شيءَ مِن الإنسانِ حجرٌ».

Q   What is the contradictory of the affirmative particular (*naqīḍ* of the *mūjabah juz'iyyah*)?

A   Its contradictory is the negative universal (*sālibah kulliyyah*). Such as "Some humans are rocks": its contradictory is "No human is a rock."

س   ما نَقيضُ السالبةِ الكلّيّةِ؟

ج   نَقيضُها الموجبةُ الجزئيّةُ، نحوُ: «لا شيءَ مِن الإنسانِ بحجرٍ» نَقيضُه «بعضُ الإنسانِ حجرٌ».

Q   What is the contradictory of the negative universal (*naqīḍ* of the *sālibah kulliyyah*)?

A   Its contradictory is the affirmative particular (*mūjabah juz'iyyah*). Such as "No human is a rock": its contradictory is "Some humans are rocks."

س   ما نَقيضُ السالبةِ الجزئيّةِ؟

ج   نَقيضُها الموجبةُ الكلّيّةُ، نحوُ: «ليسَ بعضُ الإنسانِ بحيوانٍ» نَقيضُه «كلُّ إنسانٍ حيوانٌ».

Q   What is the contradictory of the negative particular (*naqīḍ* of the *sālibah juz'iyyah*)?

A   Its contradictory is the affirmative universal (*mūjabah kulliyyah*), such as "It is not that some people are animals": its contradictory is "Every human is an animal."

(العَكسُ)(١٤٦)

5.3 CONVERSION[144]

س   ما هو العَكسُ؟

ج   هــو أن يَجعَــلَ المَوضوعَ مَحمولًا والمَحمــولَ مَوضوعًا مع بقاءٍ(١٤٧)
الإيجابِ والسلبِ بحيثُ تبقى القضيّةُ صادقةً.

Q   What is *conversion* (*'aks*)?

A   It is making the subject the predicate and the predicate the
subject, while preserving[148] the affirmative and negative, such
that the proposition remains truthful.

س   ما المرادُ ببقاءِ القضيّةِ صادقةٌ؟

ج   المرادُ بذلك أنّه لو صَدَقَت القضيّةُ صَدَقَ عكسُها.

---

144   Al-Fādānī: Know that *conversion* (*'aks*), according to them, has three types:
conversion by a concordant contradictory, conversion by a discordant contradictory, and *simple conversion* (*'aks mustawī*). I have limited myself here
to the last type because it is more frequently used, and it is what is meant
when conversion is mentioned without qualification.

145   Al-Fādānī: Know that conversion (*'aks*), according to them, has three types:
conversion by a concordant contradictory, conversion by a discordant contradictory, and simple conversion (*'aks mustawī*). I have limited myself here
to the last type because it is more frequently used, and it is what is meant
when conversion is mentioned without qualification.

١٤٦   اعلم أنّ العكس عندهم ثلاثة أنواع: عكس نقيض موافق، وعكس نقيض مخالف، وعكس
مستو، وعلى النوع الأخير اقتصرت هنا؛ لأنّه أكثر استعمالًا وهو المراد به إذا أطلق العكس.

١٤٧   قد علمت أنّ المهملة في حكم الجزئيّة على الصحيح، وعليه فالموجبة منها تعكس جزئيّةً موجبةً
، نحو «زيد حيوان»، عكسه «بعض الحيوان زيد»، والسالبة منها لا تنعكس مطّردًا كالجزئيّة
السالبة، وأمّا الشخصيّة فليست تدخل في العلوم، بل في الصناعات والعادات.

148   Al-Fādānī: You have learned that the *indeterminate proposition* (*muhmal*) is,
according to the correct view, treated as a particular proposition. Accordingly,
its affirmative can be converted into a particular affirmative, such as "Zayd
is an animal," whose conversion would be "Some animal is Zayd." As for the
negative, it does not convert restrictively like a particular negative. As for
the *personal* (*shakhṣī*) proposition, it does not pertain to the sciences, but
rather to crafts and customs.

Q   What is intended by the proposition remaining truthful?

A   The intent of that is that if the proposition was truthful, its conversion is truthful.

س   متى يكونُ العكسُ لازِمًا مُطَّرِدًا؟

ج   يكونُ مطَّرِدًا لكلِّ قضيّةٍ لم تجتمع فيها خِسَّتانِ؛ الجزءُ والسلبُ.
وهي ثلاثةُ أنواعٍ:
١ .   موجبةٌ كلّيّةٌ،
٢ .   موجبةٌ جزئيّةٌ،
٣ .   سالبةٌ كلّيّةٌ.

Q   When is a conversion consistent (*lāzim*) and restrictive (*muṭṭarid*)?

A   It is restrictive to each proposition that does not combine two basenesses (*khissatān*): the part (*al-juz'*) or the negative (*al-salb*).

It is of three types.

1.   affirmative universal (*mūjabah kulliyyah*),
2.   affirmative particular (*mūjabah juz'iyyah*), and
3.   negative universal (*sālibah kulliyyah*)

س   ما عكسُ الموجبةِ الكلّيّةِ؟

ج   عكسُها الموجبةُ الجزئيّةُ، نحوُ: «كلُّ إنسانٍ حيوانٌ» عكسُه «بعضُ الحيوانِ إنسانٌ».

Q   What is the conversion of the affirmative universal (*mūjabah kulliyyah*)?

A   Its conversion is an affirmative particular (*mūjabah juz'iyyah*). Such as "Every human is an animal": its conversion is "Some animals are human."

س   ما عكسُ الموجبةِ الجزئيّةِ؟

ج   [عكسُه موجبةٌ جزئيّةٌ كنفسِه، نحوُ: «بعضُ الإنسانِ حيوانٌ».]
عكسُه «بعضُ الحيوانِ إنسانٌ».

Q   What is the conversion of the affirmative particular (*mūjabah juz'iyyah*)?

A   [Its conversion is an affirmative particular (*mūjabah juz'iyyah*), like itself. Such as "Some humans are animals":] its conversion is "Some animals are human."

س   ما عكسُ السالبةِ الكلّيّةِ؟

ج   عكسُها سالبةٌ كلّيّةٌ كنفسِها، نحوُ: «لا شيءَ مِن الإنسانِ بحجرٍ» عكسُه «لا شيءَ مِن الحجرِ بإنسانٍ».

Q   What is the conversion of the negative universal (*sālibah kulliyyah*)?

A   Its conversion is a negative universal (*sālibah kulliyyah*) like itself. Such as "No human is a rock": its conversion is "No rock is human."

س   ما هي القضيّةُ التي لا تنعكسُ؟

ج   هي السالبةُ الجزئيّةُ، نحوُ: «بعضُ الإنسانِ ليسَ بحجرٍ»، فإنّها لا تنعكسُ عكسًا مطّردًا لا سالبةً جزئيّةً ولا سالبةً كلّيّةً، فلا يُقالُ في المثالِ المذكورِ: «كلُّ حجرٍ ليسَ بإنسانٍ»، وقد تنعكسُ عكسًا غيرَ مطّردٍ كنفسِها فيُقالُ في المثالِ المذكورِ: «بعضُ الحجرِ ليسَ بإنسانٍ».

Q   What proposition does not convert?

A   It is the negative particular (*sālibah juz'iyyah*). Such as: "Some humans are not rocks." since it does not have a consistent conversion: neither negative particular (*sālibah juz'iyyah*) nor negative universal (*sālibah kulliyyah*). Thus, it is not said for the aforementioned example [that] "Every rock is not a human." It might have an inconsistent conversion [which is] like itself. Hence, it is said for the aforementioned example: "Some rocks are not human."

6

THE PURPOSES OF ASSENTS

SYLLOGISMS & THEIR MATTERS

مقاصِدُ التصديقاتِ: الأقيِسَةُ. موادُّها.

6.1 SYLLOGISM

(القياسُ)

س ما هو القياسُ؟

ج هو قولٌ مُؤَلَّفٌ مِن قَضايا يَلزَمُ مِن تسليمِها بالضرورةِ قضيّةٌ أُخرى،
وله مـادّةٌ وصورةٌ[149]، ويُسـمَّى أيضًـا «دلـيلًا»[150] عندَهم، نحوُ
قولِنا: «العالَمُ حادثٌ، وكلُّ حادثٍ له صانعٌ»، فهاتانِ قضيّتانِ يَلزَمُ
مِن تسليمِهما ضرورةً قضيّةٌ أُخرى، هي قولُنا: «العالَمُ له صانعٌ».

---

149 من المعلوم أن كل شيء له مادة وصورة، فمادة البيت المبني الحجر والخشب والحديد والسمنت
وما أشبه ذلك، وهكَذا القياس له «مادة وصورة»: فمادته هي: القضايا، وصورته هي: هيئة
التأليف منها ومن الأشكال الأربعة الآتية.

150 فالدليل عند المناطقة، حيث فُسِّر بما ذُكر، لا بد في جميعه من تَرَكُّبه من مقدمتين
«صغرى وكبرى»، وهما كشاهدين عند الحاكم في اعتبارِهما لتحصيل المطلوب، إلا أن
الدليل يستحيل أن يكون أقلَّ منهما أو أكثر، بخلافْ حكم الحاكم، فلا يستحيل أن
يكون بأقل من اثنين أو أكثر؛ لثبوت رمضان بشاهد واحد، وثبوت الزنا بأربعة.
وأما الدليل عند الأصوليين: فهو ما يمكن التوصل بصحيح النظر فيه إلى مطلوب خبري،
«كالناظر» للصانع، و«الكتاب والسنة والإجماع» للأحكام، فهو مفرد لا يحتاج إلى
مقدمتين.

78

Q   What is a *syllogism* (*qiyās*)?

A   It is a statement composed of propositions whose concession necessarily entails another proposition. It has a material (*māddah*) and a form (*ṣūrah*).[151] According to them [the logicians], it is also called a *proof* (*dalīl*).[152] Such as "The world is contingent" and "All that is contingent has a creator" since conceding those two propositions necessarily entails another proposition, which is: "The world has a creator."

س   ما هي نتيجةُ القياسِ؟

ج   هي قضيّةٌ لَزِمَت مِن تسليمِ قضايا قياسٍ، وتُسمّى أيضًا «مطلوبًا».

Q   What is the *deduced conclusion* (*natījah*) of the syllogism?

A   It is a proposition entailed from conceding the propositions of a syllogism. It is also called the *desired conclusion* (*maṭlūb*).

س   إلى كَمْ يَنقسمُ القياسُ باعتبارِ الصورةِ؟

---

151   Al-Fādīnī: It is known that everything has both *matter* and *form* (*māddah, ṣūrah*). For example, the matter of a constructed house consists of stone, wood, iron, cement, and similar materials. Likewise, a syllogism has both *matter* and *form*: its matter is the propositions, and its form is the structure of their composition, which follows the coming four figures of syllogism.

152   Al-Fādānī: For the logicians, proof (*dalīl*)—when defined as previously mentioned—must necessarily consist of two premises, a *minor premise* (*ṣughrā*) and a *major premise* (*kubrā*). These are akin to witnesses before a judge in their role for achieving the desired conclusion. However, proof cannot be less than or more than two premises, unlike a judge's ruling, which can be based on fewer or more witnesses. For example, the confirmation of Ramadan can occur with one witness, while the proof of fornication requires four witnesses.

   As for evidence according to the legal theorists (*uṣūlīs*), it is that which, through correct reasoning, can lead to a factual conclusion, such as the world being evidence for the existence of the Creator, and the Quran, the Sunnah, and consensus being evidence for legal rulings. This type of evidence is *singular* (*mufrad*) and does not require two premises.

ج   يَنقسِمُ إلى قسمَينِ: قياسٌ اقترانيٌّ، وقياسٌ اِستِثنَائيٌّ.

Q   The syllogism, with respect to form (*ṣūrah*), divides into how many divisions?

A   It divides into two divisions:
   1. combinatorial syllogism (*qiyās iqtirānī*) and
   2. exceptive syllogism (*qiyās istithnā'ī*).

س   ما هو القياسُ الاقترانيُّ؟

ج   هو قياسٌ لا تُذكَرُ معه النتيجةُ ولا نَقيضُها بالفعلِ⁽¹⁰³⁾، نحوُ قولِنا: «كلُّ جِسمٍ مؤلَّفٍ حادثٌ؛ فكلُّ جِسمٍ حادثٌ»، فهذه النتيجةُ لم تُذكَر بهيئتِها الاجتماعيّةِ في القياسِ، بل ذُكِرَت فيه متفرّقةً.

Q   What is a *combinatorial syllogism* (*qiyās iqtirānī*)?

A   It is a syllogism which does not mention the conclusion or its contradiction in actuality.[154] Such as our statement "Every composite body is contingent. Thus, every body is contingent" since this conclusion, in its combined form, is not mentioned in the syllogism. Instead, it is mentioned separately.

س   لِمَ سُمّيَ اقترانيًّا؟

ج   لاقترانِ الحُـدودِ الثلاثةِ فيه بلا استثناءٍ، وهي: الأصغرُ والأوسطُ والأكبرُ.

---

١٠٣   وقد يسمى هذا القسم أيضًا قياسا حمليًّا؛ إذ لا فائدة فيه إلا من الحملية، وأما من الشرطية فلا جدوى فيه؛ ولهذا قال صاحب السلم «واختص بالحملية»، فمثاله من الشرطيات «كلما كان الإنسان ناطقًا كان حيوانًا و «كلما كان حيوانًا كان جسمًا» فـ «كلما كان الإنسان ناطقًا كان جسمًا».

154   Al-Fādānī: This type is also called *categorical syllogism* (*qiyās ḥamlī*), as its benefit lies only in the categorical proposition, and not in the conditional proposition, which has no utility here. This is why the author of *Al-Sullam* said, "It is specific to the categorical." An example of this from conditional propositions is: "Whenever a human is rational, he is an animal," and "Whenever an animal exists, it is a body." Therefore, "Whenever a human is rational, he is a body."

Q   Why is it called "combinatorial" (*iqtirānī*)?

A   Because the three terms are connect within it without an exceptive [operator]. They are:
1.   the minor term (*aṣghar*),
2.   the middle term (*awsaṭ*), and
3.   the major term (*akbar*).

س   ما هو الحدُّ الأصغرُ؟

ج   هو مَوضوعُ النتيجةِ، والغالبُ فيه أنّه أقلُّ أفرادًا مِن المَحمولِ.

Q   What is the *minor term* (*ḥadd aṣghar*)?

A   It is the subject of the conclusion (*mawḍuʿ al-natījah*). In most cases, it has less members than the predicate.

س   ما هو الحدُّ الأكبرُ؟

ج   هو مَحمولُ النتيجةِ، والغالبُ فيه أنّه أكثرُ أفرادًا.

Q   What is the *major term* (*ḥadd akbar*)?

A   It is the predicate of the conclusion (*maḥmūl al-natījah*). In most cases, it has more members [than the subject].

س   ما هو الحدُّ الأوسطُ؟

ج   هــو المكــرَّرُ في المقدِّمتَينِ ⁽¹⁰⁵⁾: الصُّغرى والكُبرى، فيَقَعُ متوسِّــطًا جامعًا بينَهما.

Q   What is the *middle term* (*ḥadd awsaṭ*)?

A   It is what is repeated in the two premises[156] (the minor and major). Thus, it occurs as a mediator joining between the two.

---

١٥٥   يبدو من هنا أن القياس والدليل عندهم مقدمتان فقط، وما يوجد من أكثر المقدمات فهو دليل على البعض منها على المطلوب كالقياس الذي ذكرت فيه علته.

156   Al-Fādānī: It follows from this that, according to them, a *syllogism* (*qiyās*) and a *proof* (*dalīl*) consist of only two premises. When additional premises are present, they function merely as evidence for a component of the argument that contributes to the intended conclusion—such as when the *cause* (*ʿillah*) is explicitly included within the syllogism.

س   ما هي المقدّمةُ الكُبرى؟

ج   هي قضيّة وُضِعَ فيها الحدُّ الأكبَرُ.

Q   What is the *major premise (muqaddimah kubrā)*?
A   It is a premise wherein the major term is placed.[157]

مثـالُ ذلـك قولُك «خائـنُ الأُمّـةِ مُبغَضٌ، وكلُّ مَـن أبْغَضَتْـهُ أُمّتُه لا يوَلَّـي الحكـمَ عليها إذا كانت مسـتقلّةً؛ فخائـنُ الأُمّةِ لا يولّي الحكمَ عليها إذا كانت مستقلّةً».

فمَوضوعُ هذه النتيجةِ «خائنُ الأُمّةِ» وهو الحدُّ الأصغرُ، ومَحمولُها «لا يوَلَّـى الحكـمَ الخ» وهـو الحدُّ الأكبرُ، والمقدِّمـةُ الأُولى التي فيها الحدُّ الأصغرُ مقدِّمةٌ صُغرى. والمقدِّمةُ الثانيّةُ التي فيها الحدُّ الأكبرُ مقدِّمةٌ كُبرى، والمكرَّرُ وهو «مُبغَضٌ» هو الحدُّ الأوسطُ،

An example of this is you saying:
(1) A traitor to the Ummah is despised.
(2) All whom the Ummah despise is not given authority over them when it [the Ummah] is independent.
(3) Thus, a traitor of the Ummah is not given authority over them when it [the Ummah] is independent.
Thus, the subject of this conclusion is "A traitor to the Ummah."
It is the minor term (*ḥadd aṣghar*).
Its predicate is "not given authority…." It is the major term (*ḥadd akbar*).
The first premise ["A traitor to the Ummah is despised"] which contains the minor term is the minor premise (*ṣughrā*).

---

157   (Tr:) He does not define the *minor premise (muqaddimah ṣughrā)*, perhaps expecting the reader to define it by analogy from the major premise, namely: a *minor premise (muqaddimah ṣughrā)* is one wherein the minor term is placed.

The second premise ["All whom the Ummah despise is not given authority over them when it is independent"] which contains the major term is the major premise (*kubrā*).
What is repeated (which is: "despised") is the middle term (*wusṭā*).

وهيئةُ التأليفِ مِن المقدِّمتَينِ هي صورةُ القياسِ، وتُسمّى «شَكلًا».

The compositional form of the two premises is the form of the syllogism. It is called [its] *figure* (*shakl*).

س   ما هو الشكلُ؟

ج   هو عبارةٌ عن المقدِّمتَينِ الصُّغرى والكُبرى باعتبارِ هيئةِ الوسطِ مع الأصغرِ والأكبرِ.

Q   What is the *figure* (*al-shakl*)?
A   It refers to the two premises—the minor and major (*ṣughrā* and *kubrā*)—with respect to the form of the middle (*wusṭā*) with the minor and major terms (*aṣghar* and *akbar*).

س   ما هو الضَّربُ؟

ج   هو عبارةٌ عن المقدِّمتَينِ باعتبارِ كَمِّهما وكَيفِهما.

Q   What is the *mood* (*ḍarb*)?
A   It refers to the two premises with respect to their quantity (*kamm*) and quality (*kayf*).

س   ما حُكمُ القياسِ الاقترانيِّ باعتبارِ الإنتاجِ؟

ج   حُكمُه أن تُحذَفَ الحدُّ الأوسطُ مِن مقدِّمتَيه فتَبقى النتيجةُ مِن الحدَّينِ الأصغرِ والأكبرِ.

Q   What is the rule for the combinatorial syllogism (*qiyās iqtirānī*) with respect to producing [a conclusion]?

A   Its rule is that the middle term (*ḥadd awsaṭ*) is deleted from the two premises so the conclusion remains [and, thus, composed] from the minor and major terms (*aṣghar* and *akbar*).

س   ما حُكمُ نتيجةِ القياسِ الاقترانيِّ كَمًّا وكَيفًا؟

ج   حُكمُها أنّها تتبعُ أخسَّ المقدّمتَينِ في الكَمِّ والكَيفِ، فإذا كانت إحداهما سالبةً والأُخرى موجبةً كانت النتيجةُ سالبةً، وإذا كانت إحداهما جزئيّةً والأُخرى كلّيّةً كانت النتيجةُ جزئيّةً؛ لأنّ السلبَ أخسُّ مِن الإيجابِ والجزئيَّ أخسُّ مِن الكلّيِّ.

Q   What is the rule for the combinatorial syllogism (*al-qiyās al-iqtirānī*) with respect to the quantity (*kamm*) and quality (*kayf*)?

A   Its rule is that it follows the lesser of the two premises in the[ir] quantity (*kamm*) and quality (*kayf*).
Hence:
— If one of them is negative (*sālibah*) and the other affirmative (*mūjabah*), the conclusion is negative.
— If one of them is particular (*juz'iyyah*) and the other universal (*kulliyyah*), the conclusion is negative.

[This is] because negative is lesser than affirmative, and particular is lesser than universal.

س   كَمْ أشكالُ القياسِ الاقترانيِّ؟

ج   أشكالُه أربعةٌ، ولكلِّ شكلٍ مِنها خاصّيّةٌ، وشرطُ إنتاجٍ، وضُروبٌ منتجةٌ(١٥٨).

---

١٥٨   اعلم أن كل شكل مِن الأشكال الأربعة ضروبه بحسب القسمة العقلية ستة عشر، فالضروب الممكنة للأشكال الأربعة ٦٤، غير أن المنتجة منه ٢٢ ضربًا، الشكل الأول ٤، وللشكل الثاني ٤، وللشكل الثالث ٦، وللشكل الرابع ٨، وهي التي ذكرتها هنا، وما سوى ذلك وهي ٤٢ ضربًا

Q   How many figures (*shakl*, pl. *ashkāl*) are there for the combinatorial syllogism (*qiyās iqtirānī*)?

A   It has four figures. Each of its figures have
    –   constraints (*khāṣiyyah*),
    –   conditions for producing a conclusion (*shurūṭ intāj*), and
    –   productive forms (*ḍurūb muntijah*).[159, 160]

س   ما خاصّيّةُ الشكلِ الأوّلِ؟

ج   خاصّيّتُه أن يكونَ الحـدُّ الأوسطُ مَحمولًا في الصُّغرى مَوضوعًا
    في الكُبرى، نحوُ: «العالَمُ متغيِّرٌ، وكلُّ متغيِّرٍ حـادثٌ، فالعالَمُ
    حادثٌ».

Q   What are the constraints of the first figure (*al-shakl al-awwal*)?

A   Its constraint is that the middle term is a predicate in the minor
    term and subject in the major term. Such as:
    (1) The world is a changing thing.
    (2) All changing things are contingent.
    (3) Thus, the world is contingent.

س   ما شرطُ إنتاج الشكلِ الأوّلِ؟

ج   شـرطُه أن تكـونَ الصُّغرى موجبـةً والكُبرى كلّيّـةً، فيُنتِجُ المَطالِبَ
    الأربعةَ[(١٦١)].

فضروب عقيمة غير منتجة.

159 Al-Fādānī: Know that each of the four *figures of syllogism* (*ashkāl*) has, according to rational division, sixteen possible *moods* (*ḍurūb*). Therefore, the
     total number of possible moods across the four figures is 64. However, only
     twenty-two of these moods produce valid conclusions. For the first figure,
     there are four valid moods, for the second figure, four, for the third figure,
     six, and for the fourth figure, eight. These are the ones mentioned here. The
     remaining forty-two moods are barren, non-productive moods that do not
     yield valid conclusions.

160 A summary of the figures and moods is presented in Figure 1 on page 95.

١٦١ هي: الإيجاب الكلي، والسلب الكلي، والإيجاب الجزئي، والسلب الجزئي، ومن هذا الشرط
     علِم أن خاص الخاص للشكل الأول الذي لا يشارك فيه سواه من الأشكال أنه لا يكون في

Q What are the conditions for the first figure producing a conclusion?

A Its conditions are that:
— the minor premise is affirmative, and
— the major premise is universal.

Then it will produce the four sought-after conclusions.[162]

س كَمْ الضُّروبُ المنتجةُ للشكلِ الأوّلِ؟

ج ضُروبُه المنتجةُ حَسبَ الشرطِ المذكورِ أربعةٌ[163]:

١. موجبتانِ كلّيّتانِ،

٢. موجبتانِ كُبراهما كلّيّةٌ،

٣. كلّيّتانِ كُبراهما سالبةٌ،

٤. الصُّغرى موجبةٌ جزئيّةٌ والكُبرى سالبةٌ كلّيّةٌ.

Q How many productive moods are there for the first figure?

A The productive moods according to the aforementioned conditions are four:[164]

مقدماته سالبة جزئية.

162 Al-Fādānī: They are: universal affirmative, universal negative, particular affirmative, and particular negative. From this condition, it is understood that the unique characteristic of the first figure, which no other figure shares, is that its premises cannot include a particular negative proposition.

١٦٣ فالضرب الأول نتيجته كلية موجبة: نحو: «كل إنسان حيوان» و «وكل حيوان جسم» فـ «كل إنسان جسم»، والثاني نتيجته موجبة جزئية: نحو: «بعض الوضوء عبادة» و «كل عبادة تفتقر إلى نية» فـ «بعض الوضوء يفتقر إلى نية»، والثالث نتيجته سالبة كلية: نحو: «كل وضوء عبادة» و «لا شيء من العبادة بمستغن عن النية» فـ «لا شيء من الوضوء بمستغن عن النية»، والرابع نتيجته سالبة جزئية: نحو: «بعض الوضوء عبادة» و «لا شيء من العبادة بمستغن عن النية» فـ «ليس بعض الوضوء بمستغن عن النية».

164 Al-Fādānī: The first mood results in a universal affirmative conclusion, as in: "Every human is an animal," and "Every animal is a body," thus "Every human is a body."

1. Two affirmative universals.
2. Two affirmatives, their major [premise] being universal.
3. Two universals, their major [premise] being negative.
4. The minor [premise] is an affirmative particular, the major [premise] is a negative universal.

س   ما خاصّيّةُ الشكلِ الثاني؟

ج   خاصّيّتُه أن يكونَ الحدُّ الأوسطُ مَحمولًا في المقدّمتَينِ الصُّغرى والكُبرى، نحوُ: «كلُّ إنسانٍ حيوانٌ، ولا شيءَ مِن الحجرِ بحيوانٍ؛ فلا شيءَ مِن الإنسانِ بحجرٍ».

Q   What are the constraints of the second figure (*al-shakl al-thānī*)?

A   Its constraint is that the middle term is predicated in the minor and major premises. Such as:
(1) Every human is an animal.
(2) No rock is an animal.
(3) Thus, no human is a rock.

س   ما شرطُ إنتاجِ الشكلِ الثاني؟

ج   شرطُه أن لا تَتَشابَه المقدِّمتانِ سـلبًا وإيجابًا، بل إحداهما سـالبةٌ والأُخرى موجبةٌ، فلا يُنتِجُ إلّا سالبةً.

Q   What are the conditions for the second figure producing a conclusion?

The second mood results in a particular affirmative conclusion, as in: "Some parts of ablution are acts of worship," and "Every act of worship requires intention," thus "Some parts of ablution require intention."

The third mood results in a universal negative conclusion, as in: "Every ablution is an act of worship," and "No act of worship is independent of intention," thus "No ablution is independent of intention."

The fourth mood results in a particular negative conclusion, as in: "Some parts of ablution are acts of worship," and "No act of worship is independent of intention," thus "Some parts of ablution are not independent of intention."

A   Its condition is
— that the two premises are not similar in [both being] negative and affirmative. Instead, one is negative and the other affirmative.

Hence, it does not produce except [what is] negative.

س   كَمْ الضُّروبُ المنتجةُ للشكلِ الثاني؟

ج   ضُروبُه المنتجةُ حَسبَ الشرطِ المذكورِ أربعةٌ^(١٦٥) أيضًا،

١. كلّيّتانِ كُبراهما سالبةٌ،

٢. كلّيّتانِ كُبراهما موجبةٌ،

٣. الصُّغرى موجبةٌ جزئيّةٌ والكُبرى سالبةٌ كلّيّةٌ،

٤. الصُّغرى سالبةٌ جزئيّةٌ والكُبرى موجبةٌ كلّيّةٌ.

Q   How many productive moods are there for the second figure?
A   The productive moods according to the aforementioned conditions are also four:[166]

---

١٦٥ أي: كالشكل الأول، فالضرب الأول من الشكل الثاني نتيجته كلية سالبة، نحو: «كل إنسان حيوان» و«لا شيء من الحجر بحيوان»، فلا شيء من الإنسان بحجر، والثاني نتيجته كلية سالبة أيضًا، نحو: «لا شيء من الحجر بحيوان» و«كل إنسان حيوان»، فلا شيء من الحجر بإنسان، والثالث نتيجته جزئية سالبة، نحو: «بعض الحيوان إنسان» و«لا شيء من الحجر بإنسان»، فبعض الحيوان ليس بحجر، والرابع نتيجته جزئية سالبة أيضًا، نحو: «بعض الحيوان ليس بإنسان» و«كل ناطق إنسان»، فبعض الحيوان ليس بناطق.

166 Al-Fādānī: Like the first figure, the first mood of the second figure results in a universal negative conclusion, as in: "Every human is an animal," and "No stone is an animal," thus "No human is a stone."

The second mood also results in a universal negative conclusion, as in: "No stone is an animal," and "Every human is an animal," thus "No stone is a human."

The third mood results in a particular negative conclusion, as in: "Some animals are humans," and "No stone is a human," thus "Some animals are not stones."

The fourth mood also results in a particular negative conclusion, as in: "Some animals are not humans," and "Every rational being is a human," thus "Some animals are not rational beings."

1. Two universals, their major [premise] being negative.
2. Two universals, their major [premise] being affirmative.
3. The minor [premise] is an affirmative particular, the major [premise] is a negative universal.
4. The minor [premise] is a negative particular, the major [premise] is an affirmative universal.

س   ما خاصّيّةُ الشكلِ الثالثِ؟

ج   خاصّيّتُه أن يكونَ الحدُّ الأوسطُ مَوضوعًا فـي المقدّمتَينِ، نحوُ: «كلُّ إنسانٍ حيوانٌ، وكلُّ إنسانٍ ناطقٌ؛ فبعضُ الحيوانِ ناطقٌ».

Q   What are the constraints of the third figure (*al-shakl al-thālith*)?

A   Its constraint is that the middle term is a subject in the two premises. Such as:
(1) Every human is an animal.
(2) Every human is rational.
(3) Thus, some animals are rational.

س   ما شرطُ إنتاجِ الشكلِ الثالثِ؟

ج   شـرطُه أن تكـونَ المقدّمـةُ الصُّغـرى موجبـةً، وأن تكـونَ إحـدى المقدّمتَينِ كلّيّةً فلا يُنتِجُ إلّا جزئيّةً(١٦٧).

Q   What are the conditions for the third figure producing a conclusion?

A   Its conditions are:
— that the minor premise is affirmative and
— that one of the premises is universal.
Hence, it will not produce except for [what is] particular.[168]

س   كَمْ الضُّروبُ المنتِجةُ للشكلِ الثالثِ؟

---

١٦٧   كما أن الشكل الثاني لا ينتج إلا سالبة.

168   Al-Fādānī: Just as the second figure only produces negative conclusions.

ج   ضُروبُه المنتجةُ حَسبَ الشرطِ المذكورِ سِتّةٌ(١٦٩):

١.   موجبتانِ كلّيّتانِ،

٢.   كلّيّتانِ كُبراهما سالبةٌ،

٣.   موجبتانِ صُغراهما جزئيّةٌ،

٤.   موجبتانِ والكُبرى جزئيّةٌ،

٥.   الصُّغرى موجبةٌ جزئيّةٌ والكُبرى سالبةٌ كلّيّةٌ،

٦.   الصُّغرى موجبةٌ كلّيّةٌ والكُبرى سالبةٌ جزئيّةٌ.

Q   How many productive moods are there for the third figure?

A   The productive moods, according to the aforementioned conditions, are six:[170]

<hr>

١٦٩   الضرب الأول منها ينتج موجبه: نحو: «كل حيوان جسم» و «كل حيوان نام» فـ «بعض الجسم نام». والثاني ينتج سالبة جزئية: نحو: «كل إنسان حيوان» و «لا شيء من الإنسان بفرس» فـ «بعض الحيوان ليس بفرس». والثالث ينتج موجبة جزئية: نحو: «بعض الحيوان إنسان» و «كل حيوان جسم» فـ «بعض الإنسان جسم». والرابع ينتج موجبه جزئية أيضًا: نحو «كل إنسان حيوان» و «بعض الإنسان جسم» فـ «بعض الحيوان جسم». والخامس ينتج سالبة جزئية: نحو «بعض مجهول الصفة غائب» و «لا شيء من مجهول الصفة يصح بيعه» فـ «بعض الغائب ليس هو يصح بيعه». والسادس ينتج سالبة جزئية أيضًا: نحو «كل حيوان جسم» و «بعض الحيوان ليس بفرس» فـ «بعض الجسم ليس بفرس». وبالجملة فثلاثة منها تنتج موجبة جزئية، وثلاثة أخرى تنتج سالبة جزئية.

170   Al-Fādānī: The first mood of the third figure produces a particular affirmative conclusion, as in: "Every animal is capable of growth," and "Every animal is a living being," thus "Some bodies are capable of growth."

    The second mood produces a particular negative conclusion, as in: "Every human is an animal," and "No human is a horse," thus "Some animals are not horses."

    The third mood produces a particular affirmative conclusion, as in: "Some animals are humans," and "Every animal is a body," thus "Some humans are bodies."

    The fourth mood also produces a particular affirmative conclusion, as in: "Every human is an animal," and "Some humans are bodies," thus "Some animals are bodies."

    The fifth mood produces a particular negative conclusion, as in: "Some unknown-quality items are absent," and "No unknown-quality item can be sold," thus "Some absent items cannot be sold."

1. Two affirmative universals.
2. Two universals, their major [premise] being negative.
3. Two affirmatives, their minor [premise] being particular.
4. Two affirmatives, their major [premise] being particular.
5. The minor [premise] being an affirmative particular, and the major [premise] being a negative universal.
6. The minor [premise] being an affirmative universal, and the major [premise] being a negative particular.

س   ما خاصّيّةُ الشكلِ الرابعِ؟

ج   خاصّيّتُـه أن يكـونَ الحـدُّ الأوسـطُ مَوضوعًا في الصُّغرى مَحمولًا في الكُبرى، نحوُ: «كلُّ إنسانٍ حيوانٌ، وكلُّ ناطقٍ إنسانٌ؛ فبعضُ الحيوانِ ناطقٌ».

Q   What are the constraints of the fourth figure (*al-shakl al-rābiʿ*)?

A   Its constraint is that the middle term is a subject in the minor term and a predicate in the major term. Such as:
   (1) Every human is an animal.
   (2) Every rational [being] is a human.
   (3) Thus, some animals are rational.

س   ما شرطُ إنتاجِ الشكلِ الرابعِ؟

ج   شرطُه أحدُ أَمرَينِ:

١. أن تكونَ المقدِّمتانِ موجبتَينِ مع كلّيّةِ الصُّغرى،

٢. أن تكونـا مختلفتَينِ بالإيجابِ والسـلبِ مـع كلّيّةِ إحداهما، فلا يُنتِجُ الإيجابَ الكلّيَّ (١٧١).

The sixth mood also produces a particular negative conclusion, as in: "Every animal is a body," and "Some animals are not horses," thus "Some bodies are not horses."

In summary, three of these moods produce particular affirmative conclusions, and the other three produce particular negative conclusions.

١٧١ أي: وينتج ثلاثة مطالب، أعني: الإيجاب الجزئي، والسلب الجزئي، والسلب الكلي.

Q   What are the conditions for the fourth figure producing a conclusion?

A   Its conditions are one of two things:
1.   The premises being affirmative and the minor [premise] being universal.
2.   That they differ in being affirmative and negative, with one of them being universal.

Hence, it will not produce the affirmative universal.[172]

س   كَمْ الضُروبُ المنتجةُ للشكلِ الرابعِ؟

ج   ضُروبُه المنتجةُ حَسبَ الشرطِ المذكورِ ثمانيّةٌ[173]:

١.   موجبتانِ كلّيّتانِ،

٢.   موجبتانِ كُبراهما جزئيّةٌ،

٣.   كلّيّتانِ كُبراهما موجبةٌ،

٤.   كلّيّتانِ كُبراهما سالبةٌ،

٥.   الصُّغرى موجبةٌ جزئيّةٌ والكُبرى سالبةٌ،

٦.   الصُّغرى سالبةٌ جزئيّةٌ والكُبرى موجبةٌ كلّيّةٌ،

٧.   الصُّغرى موجبةٌ كلّيّةٌ والكُبرى سالبةٌ جزئيّةٌ،

٨.   الصُّغرى سالبةٌ كلّيّةٌ والكُبرى موجبةٌ جزئيّةٌ.

---

172   Al-Fādānī: That is, it produces three types of conclusions, namely: particular affirmative, particular negative, and universal negative.

١٧٣   فالضرب الأول ينتج موجبة جزئية: نحو: «كل إنسان حيوان» و«كل ناطق إنسان» فـ«بعض الحيوان ناطق». والثاني ينتج موجبة جزئية أيضًا: نحو: «كل إنسان حيوان» و«بعض الناطق إنسان» فـ«بعض الحيوان ناطق». والثالث ينتج سالبة كلية: نحو: «لا شيء من العبادة بمستغن عن النية» و«كل وضوء عبادة» فـ«لا شيء من المستغني عن النية بوضوء». والخمسة الباقية نتائجها سوالب جزئيات: فالرابع نحو: «كل إنسان حيوان» و«لا شيء من الفرس بإنسان» فـ«بعض الحيوان ليس بفرس». والخامس نحو: «بعض الإنسان حيوان» و«لا شيء من الفرس بإنسان» فـ«بعض الحيوان ليس بفرس». السادس: نحو: «بعض المستيقظ ليس بنائم» و«كل كاتب مستيقظ» فـ«بعض النائم ليس بكاتب». السابع: نحو: «كل كاتب متحرك الأصابع» و«بعض ساكن الأصابع ليس بكاتب» فـ«بعض متحرك الأصابع ليس بساكن الأصابع». الثامن: نحو: «لا شيء من المتحرك بساكن» و«بعض المنتقل متحرك» فـ«بعض الساكن ليس بمنتقل».

Q   How many productive moods are there for the fourth figure?
A   The productive moods according to the aforementioned conditions are eight:[174]
1.   Two affirmative universals.
2.   Two affirmatives, the major [premise] being particular.
3.   Two universals, the major [premise] being affirmative.
4.   Two universals, the major [premise] being negative.
5.   The minor [premise] being an affirmative particular, the major [premise] being a negative [universal].
6.   The minor [premise] being a negative particular, the major [premise] being an affirmative universal.
7.   The minor [premise] being an affirmative universal, major [premise] being a negative particular.
8.   The minor [premise] being a negative universal, the major [premise] being an affirmative particular.

---

174   Al-Fādānī: The first mood produces a particular affirmative conclusion, such as: "Every human is an animal," and "Every rational being is a human," thus "Some animals are rational."

The second mood also produces a particular affirmative conclusion, such as: "Every human is an animal," and "Some rational beings are humans," thus "Some animals are rational."

The third mood produces a universal negative conclusion, such as: "No act of worship is independent of intention," and "Every ablution is an act of worship," thus "No act independent of intention is ablution."

The remaining five moods produce particular negative conclusions:

The fourth, for example: "Every human is an animal," and "No horse is a human," thus "Some animals are not horses."

The fifth, for example: "Some humans are animals," and "No horse is a human," thus "Some animals are not horses."

The sixth, for example: "Some awake persons are not asleep," and "Every writer is awake," thus "Some who are asleep are not writers."

The seventh, for example: "Every writer moves their fingers," and "Some who are not moving their fingers are not writers," thus "Some who move their fingers are not motionless."

The eighth, for example: "No moving being is stationary," and "Some who transition are moving," thus "Some who are stationary are not transitioning."

These moods illustrate how different types of premises in various figures produce either affirmative or negative conclusions, with varying degrees of universality and particularity.

س ما هو أكملُ الأشكالِ الأربعةِ إنتاجًا؟

ج أكملُها الشكلُ الأوّلُ(١٧٥)، ولـذا يُسـمّى عندَهـم بـ «الشـكلِ
الكامـلِ»؛ لأنَّـه مُنتِـجُ المطالـبِ الأربعةِ؛ ولأنَّه جـاءَ على النظمِ
الطبيعيِّ وهـو انتقالٌ مِن المَوضوعِ إلى الحدِّ الأوسطِ ثُمَّ مِنه إلى
المَحمـولِ حتّى يَلـزَمَ الانتقالُ مِن المَوضوعِ إلـى المَحمولِ لكونِه
فردًا مِن أفرادِ الوسطِ.

Q Which of the four figures is the most perfect with respect to
producing conclusions?

A The most perfect is the first;[176] this is why they [i.e. the logicians]
call it "the perfect figure." [They do so] because it produces
the four sought-after conclusions. And because it follows a
natural organisation, which is moving from the subject to the
middle term, then from it to the predicate, so it necessitates
moving from the subject to the predicate out of it being one
of the members of the middle [term].

س ما هو القياسُ الاستثنائيُّ؟

ج هـو مـا يكونُ النتيجةُ أو نَقيضُها مذكورةً فيه بالفعلِ(١٧٧)، ويُسـمّى
أيضًـا «قياسًـا شـرطيًّا»، نحوُ: «إن كانت الشـمسُ طالعـةً فالنهارُ

---

١٧٥ ولهذا كانت الأشكال الثلاثة الباقية ترد إليه، فالشكل الثاني يرد إليه بعكس المقدمة الكبرى،
والشكل الثالث بعكس المقدمة الصغرى، والشكل الرابع إما بعكس المقدمتين الصغرى والكبرى،
وإما بعكس الترتيب، فتجعل المقدمة الصغرى مكان الكبرى، وتجعل الكبرى مكان الصغرى.

176 Al-Fādānī: For this reason, the remaining three figures can be reduced to
the first figure. The second figure is reduced to it by converting the major
premise; the third by converting the minor premise; and the fourth either
by converting both the minor and the major premises or by changing the
order, placing the minor premise in the position of the major and the major
in the position of the minor.

١٧٧ بأن يكون طرفاها مذكورين فيه بالفعل نحو المثال المذكور، أو يكون طرفا نقيضها مذكورين فيه
بالفعل نحو قوله تعالى «لو كان فيهما آلهة إلا اللّه لفسدتا» والتقدير: لكنهما لم تفسدا، فلم
يكن فيهما إله غير اللّه، ومعنى الفساد: هو خروج الشيء عن حيز الاعتدال والاستواء، فضده:
الإصلاح.

FIGURE 1. Summary of Figures I–IV and Their Productive Modes

Note: minor premise precedes major premise.

Form I. The minor premise must be affirmative; the major premise must be universal.

It has four productive forms.

1   "All J are B, all B are A, so all J are A."
2   "Some J are B, all B are A, so some J are A."
3   "All J are B, no B are A, so no J are A."
4   "Some J are B, no B are A, so some J are not A."

Figure II. One premise must be affirmative and one negative; the major premise must be universal.

It also has four productive modes.

1   "All J are B, no A are B, so no J are A."
2   "No J are B, all A are B, so no J are A."
3   "Some J are B, no A are B, so some J are not A."
4   "Some J are not B, all A are B, so some J are not A."

Figure III. The major premise must be affirmative; one premise must be universal.

It has six productive modes.

1   "All B are J, all B are A, so some J are A."
2   "All B are J, no B are A, so some J are not A.
3   "Some B are J, all B are A, so some J are A."
4   "All B are J, some B are A, so some J are A."
5   "Some B are J, no B are A, so some J are not A."
6   "All B are J, some B are not A, some J are not A."

Figure IV. Either both of the premises are affirmative and the minor premise is universal; or one is affirmative and the other negative, and one premise is universal.

It has eight productive modes.

1   "All B are J, all A are B, so some J are A."
2   All B are J, some A are B, so some J are A."
3   "No B are J, all A are B, so no J are A."
4   "All B are J, no A are B, so some J are not A."
5   "Some B are J, no A are B, so some J are not A."
6   "Some B are not J, all A are B, so some J are not A."
7   "All B are J, some A are not B, so some J are not A."
8   "No B are J, some A are B, so some J are not A."

مَوجودٌ، لكـنَّ الشـمسَ طالعـةٌ؛ فالنهـارُ مَوجودٌ»، فهـذه النتيجةُ
مَذكورةٌ بهيئتِها الاجتماعيّةِ في تالي القياسِ.

Q What is an *exceptive syllogism* (*qiyās istithnā'ī*)?

A It is one where the conclusion or its contrary is mentioned
therein, in actuality.[178] It is also called a *conditional syllogism*
(*qiyās sharṭiyyah*). Such as:
(1) If the sun is risen then daytime is present.
(2) But the sun is risen.
(3) Thus, daytime is present.
Since that conclusion is mentioned in its combined form in
the consequent of the syllogism.

س إلى كَمْ يَنقسمُ القياسُ الاستثنائيُّ؟

ج يَنقسـمُ إلى قسـمَينِ: قيـاسٍ استثنائيٍّ متّصـلٍ، وقياسٍ استثنائيٍّ
منفصلٍ.

Q The exceptive syllogism (*qiyās istithnā'ī*) divides into how many
divisions?

A It divides into two divisions:
1. conjunctive exceptive syllogism (*qiyās istithnā'ī muttaṣil*)
and
2. disjunctive exceptive syllogism (*qiyās istithnā'ī munfaṣil*).

س ما هو القياسُ الاستثنائيُّ المتّصلُ؟

ج هـو قولٌ مؤلَّفٌ مِن قضيّتَينِ إحداهمـا[(١٧٩)] تتألَّفُ مِن جملتَينِ قُرِنَ

---

178 Al-Fādānī: By both terms being explicitly mentioned in it, as in the aforementioned example; or the terms of its contradictory being explicitly mentioned
in it, such as in His saying, "Had there been in them gods besides Allah, they
both would have been corrupted" (Q21:22), with the implied meaning: "But
they were not corrupted, so there was no god in them besides Allah." The
meaning of *corruption* (*fasād*) is the deviation of something from the state
of balance and order; its opposite is *rectification* (*iṣlāḥ*).

١٧٩ وتسمى كما سبق «قضية شرطية متصلة» وجملتاها حمليتان، أولاهما تسمى المقدم، وأخراهما
تسمى التالي.

بهما شرطٌ، والأُخرى قضيّةٌ واحِدَةٌ^(۱۸۰) يُقرَنُ بها كلمةُ الاستثناءِ.

Q   What is a *conjunctive exceptive syllogism* (*qiyās istithnā'ī muttaṣil*)?

A   It is a statement composed of two propositions. The first of them[181] consists of two sentences joined by a condition. The other is a single proposition[182] joined with an exceptive word (*kalimat al-istithnā'*).

س   ما حُكمُ القياسِ الاستثنائيِّ المتّصلِ باعتبارِ الإنتاج؟

ج   حُكمُه أن تُستَثنى عينُ المقدَّمِ أو نَقيضُ التالي. هذا إن لم يكن التالي مُساويًا للمقدَّمِ، وإلّا فلك أن تَستَثني عينَ التالي أو نَقيضَ المقدَّمِ.

Q   What is the rule for the conjunctive exceptive syllogism (*qiyās istithnā'ī muttaṣil*) with respect to production?

A   Its rule is that the premise itself or the contrary of the consequent is excluded. This is if the consequent is not equivalent to the premise. Otherwise, you can exclude the consequent itself or the contrary of the premise.

س   ما حُكمُ نتيجةِ القياسِ الاستثنائيِّ المتّصلِ؟

ج   حُكمُها أنّ استثناءَ عينِ المقدَّمِ يُنتِجُ عينَ التالي، نحوُ: «إن كانَ هذا إنسانٌ فهو حيوانٌ، لكنّه إنسانٌ؛ فهو حيوانٌ»، وأنّ استثناءَ نَقيضِ التالي يُنتِجُ نَقيضَ المقدَّمِ، كما إذا قلنا في المثالِ المَذكورِ «لكنّه ليسَ بحيوانٍ؛ فليسَ بإنسانٍ»، ويَزيدُ ما إذا كانَ التالي

---

۱۸۰   وتسمى هذه الأخرى بالقضية الاستثنائية؛ لاشتمالها عن أداة الاستثناء أعني «لكن».

181   Al-Fādānī: As mentioned earlier, this is called a *conditional conjunctive proposition* (*qaḍiyyah sharṭiyyah muttaṣilah*), and its two parts are categorical propositions. The first part is called the *antecedent* (*muqaddam*), and the second part is called the *consequent* (*tālī*).

182   Al-Fādānī: This is referred to as the *exceptive proposition* (*qaḍiyyah istithnā'iyyah*), due to its inclusion of the exceptive operand, namely "but."

مُساوِيًا للمقدَّمِ بأنّ استثناءَ عينِ التالي يُنتِجُ عينَ المقدَّمِ، واستثناءَ نَقيضِ المقـدَّمِ يُنتِـجُ نَقيضَ التالي، نحوُ: «إذا كانت الشمسُ طالعةً كانَ النهارُ مَوجودًا، ولكنّ النهارَ مَوجودٌ؛ فالشمسُ طالعةٌ»، أو «لكنّ الشمسَ غيرُ طالعةٍ؛ فالنهارُ غيرُ مَوجودٍ»(١٨٣).

Q   What are the conditions for the conjunctive exceptive syllogism (*qiyās istithnāʾī muttaṣil*) producing a conclusion?

A   Its rule is that:
— Excluding the itself premise produces the consequent itself. Such as:

(1)   If that is a human, it is an animal.

(2a)   But it is a human.

(3a)   Thus, it is an animal.

— Excluding the contrary of the consequent produces the contrary of the premise, just as if we had said in the afore-mentioned example:

(2b)   But it is not an animal.

(3b)   Thus, it is not a human.

Additionally, when the consequent is equivalent to the premise, excluding the consequent itself produces the premise itself, and excluding the premise itself produces the contrary of consequent. Such as:

(1)   When the sun is risen, daytime is present.

(2a)   But daytime is present.

(3a)   Thus, the sun is risen.

(2b)   But the sun is not risen.

(3b)   Thus, daytime is not present."[184]

---

١٨٣   فيكون المنتج هنا أربعة أوجه، وفيما عدا ذلك المنتج وجهان فقط، والعقيم وجهان.

184 Al-Fādānī: Thus, in this case, the valid conclusion has four forms, while in other cases the valid conclusion has only two forms, and the barren one has two forms as well.

س   ما هو القياسُ الاستثنائيُّ المنفصلُ؟

ج   هـو قـولٌ مؤلَّفٌ مِن قضيَّتَيـنِ، إحداهمـا قضيَّةٌ شَـرطيَّةٌ منفصلةٌ؛
والأُخرى قضيَّةٌ استثنائيَّةٌ.

Q   What is a *disjunctive exceptive syllogism* (*qiyās istithnā'ī munfaṣil*)?

A   It is a statement composed of two propositions. The first is
a disjunctive conditional proposition (*qaḍiyyah sharṭiyyah
munfaṣilah*). The other is an exceptive syllogism (*qaḍiyyah
istithnā'iyyah*).

س   ما حُكمُ القياسِ الاستثنائيِّ المنفصلِ باعتبارِ الإنتاجِ؟

ج   إذا كانت قضيَّتُها الشرطيَّةُ المنفصلةُ حقيقيَّةً فتُستَثنى عينُ أحدِ
الطرفَينِ أو نَقيضِه، وإذا كانت مانعةَ الجمعِ فتُستَثنى عينُ أحدِهما
فقط، وإذا كانت مانعةَ الخُلوِّ فتُستَثنى نَقيضُ أحدِهما فقط.

Q   What is the rule for the disjunctive exceptive syllogism (*qiyās
istithnā'ī munfaṣil*) with respect to production?

A   When its disjunctive exceptive proposition is a literal (*ḥaqīqah*),
one of the parts itself or its contradictory is excluded.
When it is anti-combinatorial (*māni'at al-jam'*), just one of
them itself is excluded.
When it is anti-exclusionary (*māni'at al-khuluww*), just the
contradictory of one of them is excluded.

س   ما حُكمُ نتيجةِ القياسِ الاستثنائيِّ المنفصلِ؟

ج   حُكمُها أنّ استثناءَ عينِ أحدِ طرفَي قضيّتِه الشرطيَّةُ المنفصلةُ يُنتِجُ
نَقيضَ الآخَرِ، واستثناءُ نَقيضِ أحدِهما يُنتِجُ عينَ الآخَرِ (١٨٥).

---

١٨٥   فيكون المنتج في الحقيقية أربعة أوجه، وفي مانعة الجمع وجهين، والعقيم وجهان، وفي مانعة
الخلو المنتج وجهان والعقيم وجهان.

فالحقيقيّةُ، نحوُ: «العددُ إمّا زوجٌ أو فردٌ، لكنّه زوجٌ؛ فليسَ بفردٍ»،

[أو:] «لكنّه فـردٌ؛ فليسَ بزوجٍ»، أو «لكنّه ليسَ بزوجٍ؛ فهو فردٌ»،

أو «لكنّه ليسَ بفردٍ؛ فهو زوجٌ»،

ومانعةُ الجمعِ، نحوُ: «إمّا أن يكونَ الجسـمُ أبيضَ أو أسـودَ، لكنّه

أبيضُ؛ فليسَ بأسودَ» أو «لكنّه أسودُ؛ فليسَ بأبيضَ»،

ومانعةُ الخُلوِّ، نحوُ: «إمّا أن يكونَ الشيءُ غيرَ أبيضَ أو غيرَ أسودَ،

لكنّه أبيضُ؛ فهو غيرُ أسودَ»، أو «لكنّه أسودُ؛ فهو غيرُ أبيضَ».

Q What are the conditions for the disjunctive exceptive syllogism (*qiyās istithnā'ī munfaṣil*) producing a conclusion?

A Its rule is that excluding one of the parts of its disjunctive conditional proposition itself produces the contradictory of the other, and excluding the contradictory of one of them produces the other itself.[186]

The proper disjunctive (*ḥaqīqah*) is such as:

(1) A number is either even or odd.

(2–3a)   But it is even. Thus, it is not odd.

(2–3b)   But it is odd. Thus, it is not even.

(2–3c)   But it is not even. Thus, it is odd.

(2–3d)   But it is not odd. Thus, it is even.

The anti-combinatorial (*māniʿat al-jamʿ*) is such as:

(1) The body is either white or black.

(2–3a)   But it is white. Thus, it is not black.

(2–3b)   But it is black. Thus, it is not white.

The anti-exclusionary (*māniʿat al-khuluww*) is such as:

(1) The thing is either not white or not black.

---

186 Al-Fādānī: Thus, the valid conclusion in reality has four forms, while in the *anti-combinatorial* (*māniʿ al-jamʿ*), it has two forms, and the barren has two forms. In the *anti-exclusionary* (*maniʿat al-khuluw*), the valid conclusion has two forms, and the barren has two forms.

(2–3a)   But it is white. Thus, it is not black.
(2–3b)   But it is black. Thus, it is not white.

6.2 THE MATERIALS OF SYLLOGISM   مواد الأقيسةِ

س   كَمْ موادُّ الأقيسةِ؟ وإلى كَمْ تنقسمُ؟

ج   موادُّها اثنا عشر نوعًا، وتنقسمُ إلى قسمَينِ:

١.   يقينيّةٌ؛ وهي ستّةُ أنواعٍ: أوّليّاتٌ، ومشاهداتٌ، ومجرَّباتٌ، وحدسيّاتٌ، ومتواتراتٌ، ومقدِّماتٌ نظريّةٌ قياسيّةٌ.

٢.   وظنّيّةٌ؛ وهي ستّةُ أنواعٍ أيضًا: مشهوراتٌ، ومسلَّماتٌ، ومقبولاتٌ، ومُشبِّهاتٌ، ومُخيِّلاتٌ، ووهميّاتٌ.

Q   The *materials* (*māddah*, pl. *mawād*) of syllogisms are how many? And they divide [into] how many [divisions]?

A   Its materials (*mawād*) are twelve species. They divide into two divisions.

1.   *Certain* (*yaqīniyyah*). It is six species:
     a.   first principles (*awwaliyyāt*),
     b.   observables (*mushāhadāt*),
     c.   experiments (*mujarrabāt*),
     d.   intuitions (*ḥadasiyyāt*),
     e.   mass-transmitted information (*mutawātirāt*), and
     f.   primitive syllogistic conjectures (*muqaddimāt*).
2.   *Presumptive* (*ẓaniyyah*). It is also six species:
     a.   commonly known (*mashhūrāt*),
     b.   conceded (*musallamāt*),
     c.   accepted (*maqbūlāt*),
     d.   deceptions (*mushabbahāt*),
     e.   imaginings (*mukhayyilāt*), and
     f.   false imaginings (*wahmiyyāt*).

س إلى كَمْ يَنقسمُ القياسُ باعتبارِ المادّةِ؟

ج يَنقسـمُ إلى خمسـةِ أقسـامٍ: بُرهانيٌّ، وجدليٌّ، وإقناعيٌّ، وشِعريٌّ، وسوفُسطائيٌّ.

Q The syllogism, with respect to the material (*māddah*), divides into how many divisions?

A It divides into five divisions:

1. demonstrative (*burhānī*),
2. dialectical (*jadalī*),
3. persuasive (*iqnā'ī*),
4. poetic (*shi'rī*), and
5. sophistic (*sūfustā'ī*)

س ما هو القياسُ البرهانيُّ؟

ج هو قياسٌ مؤلَّفٌ مِن مقدِّماتٍ يقينيّةٍ(١٨٧)، ويُسمّى أيضًا «بُرهانًا».

Q What is a *demonstrative syllogism (qiyās burhānī)*?

A It is a syllogism comprising of premises that are certain (*yaqīniyyah*).[188] It is also called a *demonstration (burhān)*.

س إلى كَمْ يَنقسمُ البرهانُ؟

ج يَنقسمُ إلى قسمَينِ: برهانٌ لِمّيٌّ، وبرهانٌ إنّيٌّ.

Q The demonstration (*burhān*) divides into how many divisions?

A It divides into two divisions:

1. the *why-demonstration (burhān limmī)* and
2. the *if-demonstration (burhān innī)*.

---

١٨٧ وقد قدمنا آنفا أن أنواع اليقينيات ستة فكل واحدة منها لا سبيل للخطإ فيها.

188 Al-Fādānī: We have previously stated that the materials conveying certainties (*yaqīniyyāt*) are six types, and each one of them has no way of being incorrect.

س   ما هو البرهانُ اللِّمّيُّ^(١٨٩)؟

ج   هـو مـا كانَ الحدُّ الأوسـطُ فيـه عِلَّةً لثُبـوتِ الأكبـرِ للأصغرِ ذهنًا
وخارجًا، نحوُ: «خالدٌ متعفِّنُ الأخلاطِ^(١٩٠)، وكلُّ متعفِّنٍ الأخلاطِ
مَحمومٌ؛ فخالدٌ مَحمومٌ».

Q   What is a *why-demonstration* (*burhān limmī*)?[191]

A   It is one wherein the middle term is the cause for affirming the
major [premise] for the minor, mentally and extra-mentally.
Such as:

(1) Khalid has a disorder of the humours.[192]

(2) Every being having a disorder of the humours is feverish.

(3) Thus, Khalid is feverish.

س   ما هو البرهانُ الإنّيُّ^(١٩٣)؟

---

١٨٩   بتشديد الميم نسبة إلى «لم» بتخفيفها؛ لأنه يجاب به السؤال بـ «لم».

١٩٠   أي: الطبائع الأربع الموجودة فيه، وفي كل إنسان السوداء والصفراء والبلغم والدم، والمراد بتعفنها:
تغيرها وخروجها عن الاستقامة.

191   Al-Fādānī: With a doubled *mīm*, a relation to *lima* with it being lightened;
this is because it responds to questions [starting with] "Why?") *lima*.

192   Al-Fādānī: That is: the four humours present in it, and in every human
being—black bile, yellow bile, phlegm, and blood. The intended meaning
of their corruption is their alteration and deviation from normalcy.

(Tr:) This refers to Greek humourism which was the dominant system
of medicine in the West, Middle East, and India—up until the 19th century.
According to humourism, four bodily fluids affect human health, behaviour,
and personality. Hippocrates (460–370 BC) is usually credited with being
the first to write about applying humourism to medicine. He categorised the
humours as blood, phlegm, yellow bile, and black bile. Later, Galen (129–200
AD) categorised the humours as hot, cold, wet, and dry. Humourism was
adopted and developed by Muslim physicians. Perhaps the best-known
example of Muslim writings on the subjects is Ibn Sīnā (980–1037 AD)'s *The
Canon of Medicine*, which was a standard medical textbook in European
universities as late as 1650 AD.

١٩٣   بتشديد النون نسبة إلى «إن» لاقتصاره على إنية الحكم -أي: ثبوت الحكم دون لميته- من
قولهم «إن الأمر كذا».

ج   هو ما كانَ الحدُّ الأوسطُ فيه عِلَّةً لذلك الثبوتِ ذهنًا فقط، نحوُ:

«خالـدٌ مَحمـومٌ، وكلُّ مَحمـومٍ مُتَعَفِّـنُ الأخلاطِ؛ فخالـدٌ مُتَعَفِّنُ

الأخلاطِ»، فالحُمَّى عِلَّةٌ لتعفُّنِ الأخلاطِ في الذهنِ فقط.

Q   What is an *if-demonstration* (*burhān innī*)?[194]

A   It is the one wherein the middle term is the cause for affirming
that, [but] only mentally. Such as:
(1) Khalid is feverish.
(2) Every feverish [being] has a disorder of the humours.
(3) Thus, Khalid has a disorder of the humours.
Since feverishness is a cause for having a disorder of the humours, [but] only mentally.

س   ما هي اللاأوَّلِيّاتُ؟

ج   هـي المعلوماتُ التي يَحكُمُ بها العقـلُ بمجرَّدِ تصوُّرِ طرفَيها[195]،
نحوُ: «الاثنَينِ أكثرُ مِن الواحدِ»، و «ثلاثةٌ وثلاثةٌ يُساوي ستّةٌ».

Q   What are *first principles* (*awwaliyyāt*)?

A   They are the knowns that reason judges [to be true] simply
by conceptualising their two terms.[196] Such as: "Two is bigger
than one" and "Three and three equal six."

س   ما هي المُشاهداتُ؟

ج   هـي المعلومـاتُ التي لا يَحكُمُ بها العقلُ بمجرَّدِ تصوُّرِ طرفَيها بل
يَحتاجُ إلى مشاهدتِها بالحسِّ، ويُسمَّى أيضًا «محسوساتٍ»، سواءٌ

---

194   Al-Fādānī: With a doubled *nūn*, a relation to *inna*, as it is restricted to the
factuality of the judgment—that is, the establishment of the judgment without
negation—from their saying "indeed (*inna*), the matter is such-and-such."

١٩٥   وتأتي في أوائل العقول، ويستوي فيها جميع الناس.

196   Al-Fādānī: It arrises at the initial stages of intellect, and all people are alike
in it.

كانَ الحسُّ ظاهرًا، نحوُ: «الكافورُ أبيضُ»، و «الفَحمُ أسودُ»، و
«النـارُ حـارّةٌ»، و «الثلجُ باردٌ»، أو باطنًا، نحوُ قولِنا: «إنّ لنا جُوعًا
وعطشًا(١٩٧)».

Q   What are *observables* (*mushāhadāt*)?

A   They are the knowns that the mind does not judge [to be true]
    simply by conceptualisation of their two terms; instead they
    need to be observed by the senses. They are also called *sensory
    objects* (*maḥsūsāt*). It is the same whether the sense is:
    — external, such as: "camphor is white," "coal is black," "fire
      is hot," "ice is cold"; or
    — internal, such as our statement that we have hunger and
      thirst.[198]

س   ما هي المجرّباتُ؟

ج   هي التي يَحتاجُ العقلُ في الجزمِ بها إلى تكرارِ المشاهدةِ مرّةً بعدَ
    أُخرى، نحوُ(١٩٩): «المِلحُ الإنكِليزيُّ وزيتُ الخِروَعِ مسهِّلانِ».

Q   What are *experiments* (*mujarrabāt*)?

A   They are what the mind must observe repeatedly in order to
    be convinced of them. Such as:[200] "English salt and castor oil
    are laxatives."

---

١٩٧ وكذا إن لنا فكرًا وخوفًا وغضبًا وشهوةً وحزنًا وفرحًا وانقباضًا وانبساطًا وحبًّا وكراهةً وجبنًا وشجاعةً،
     وما أشبه ذلك من الصفات الباطنية التي تحس بها من تلقاء أنفسنا بدون استعانة في معرفتها
     على الحواس الظاهرة.

198 Al-Fādānī: Likewise, we have thought, fear, anger, desire, sorrow, joy, contrac-
     tion, expansion, love, hatred, cowardice, courage, and similar inner qualities
     that we perceive directly within ourselves without relying on external senses
     to know them.

١٩٩ ونحو قولنا: «ضرب الحيوان مؤلم، وحز الرقبة مهلك، والخبز مشبع، والتفاح حلو، والماء مرو،
     والنار محرقة».

200 Al-Fādānī: Similar to our statements: "Striking an animal causes pain,"
     "cutting the neck is fatal," "bread is nourishing," apples are sweet," "water
     quenches thirst," and "fire burns."

س   ما هي الحدسيّاتُ؟

ج   هي مـا يحكُمُ العقـلُ فيها بحدسٍ مِن النفس، نحـوُ: «نورُ القمرِ مستفادٌ مِن ضـوءِ الشـمسِ»؛ لِما نُشـاهِدُ أنّه إنّما هـو كالمِرآةِ يَقَـعُ ضـوءُ الشـمسِ عليـه وهو يُفيضُـه علـى الأرضِ، وكلَّما كانَ أقـربَ إليهـا قَلَّ نورُه، وكُلَّما بَعُـدَ ازدادَ النورُ، حتّى إذا قابلَها تمتَلِأُ نورًا(٢٠١).

Q   What are *intuitions* (ḥadasiyyāt)?

A   They are what the mind judges [to be true] based on self intuition. Such as "The moon's light is derived from the sun's light" due to our observing that it is like a mirror: The sun's light falls upon it and it flows upon the earth. When it [the moon] is closer to it [the sun], its [the moon's] light is reduced. When it is distant, the light increases. And when it is opposite it, it is full of light.[202]

س   ما هي المُتواتِراتُ؟

ج   هـي التـي يَحكُمُ العقـلُ فيها بواسطةِ السماعِ عن جمعٍ يُؤمَنُ تَواطؤُهـم علـى الكَذِبِ عادةً، نحوُ: «نبيُّنـا محمّدٌ [ﷺ] ظَهَرَت المعجزةُ على يدِه».

Q   What are *mass-transmitted information* (mutawātirāt)?

A   They are what reason judges [to be true] by it being heard from a group who are safe from colluding upon a lie. Such as: "Our Prophet Muḥammad [(may Allah bless him and give him peace)]: miracles manifested upon his hands."

---

٢٠١   فهذا دليل جاء للنفس بطريق الحدس أن نور القمر مستفاد من ضوء الشمس.

202   Al-Fādānī: This is argument comes to the mind through intuition, that the light of the moon is derived from the light of the sun.

س   ما هي المقدِّماتُ النظريّةُ القياسيّةُ؟

ج   هـي ما يَحكُمُ فيها العقلُ بوسطٍ قريبِ الحُضـورِ^(۲۰۳) في الذهنِ، وتُسـمّى أيضًا «قضايـا قياسـاتُها معهـا »، نحـوُ: «الإثنـانِ ثُلُثُ السـتّةِ»، فهذا معلومٌ ولكنّ علمَه بسـببِ وسطٍ حاضرٍ في الذهنِ وهو «الإثنانِ يُقسِّـمُ السـتّةَ ثلاثةَ أقسامٍ مُتساويةٍ، وكلُّ ما يَنقسمُ بعددِ ثلاثةِ أقسامٍ مُتَساويةٍ فذلك العددُ ثُلُثُه؛ فالاثنانِ ثُلُثُ السـتّةِ».

Q   What are *primitive syllogistic conjectures* (*muqaddimāt naẓariyyah qiyāsiyyah*)?

A   They are what reason judges [to be true] by a process that is [always] close[204] to mind. They are also called *propositions that provide their own syllogism*. Such as: "Two is one third of six," since this is known. But knowing it is because of a process that is [always] present in the mind which is:

(1) Two divides six into three equal portions.

(2) Everything that divides by a number into three equal portions... that number is its third.

(3) Thus, two is a third of six."

س   ما هو القياسُ الجدليُّ^(۲۰۵)؟

ج   هو قياسٌ مؤلَّفٌ مِن مقدِّماتٍ مَشهورةٍ أو مُسلَّمةٍ.

Q   What is a *dialectical syllogism* (*qiyās jadalī*)?[206]

A   It is a syllogism comprising commonly accepted (*mashhūrāt*) or conceded (*musallamāt*) premises.

---

۲۰۳   أي: لا يغيب عن ذهن جميع الناس عند تصور الطرفين.

204   Al-Fādānī: That is: it does not escape the minds of all people when conceptualising both terms of the matter.

۲۰۵   وهذا القياس نافع في مخاطبة من يقصر نظره عن البرهان.

206   Al-Fādānī: And this type of syllogism is useful in addressing those whose understanding falls short of grasping the demonstrative proof (*burhān*).

س   ما هي المشهوراتُ؟

ج   هـي مقدِّمـاتٌ اعترفت بهـا الجُمهورُ لسـببٍ مِن الأسبابِ^(٢٠٧)، كمصلحةٍ عامّةٍ، ورقّةِ القلبِ، وما جُبِلَ عليه الإنسانُ مِن الحميّةِ والأنفـةِ، فـالأوّلُ نحـوُ: «العـدلُ حسـنٌ والظلـمُ قبيـحٌ»، والثاني [نحـوُ:] «ذبـحُ الحيـوانِ قبيـحٌ»، والثالـثُ، نحوُ: «الرضا بفُجورِ امرأتِه مُستَقبَحٌ».

Q   What are *commonly known premises* (*mashhūrāt*)?

A   They are premises that the masses recognise for one of several reasons.[208] Such as:

1.   public interest (*maṣlaḥah ʿāmmah*),
2.   tender heartedness, and
3.   man's tendencies for zeal and pride.

The first is such as: "Justice is good. Oppression is bad."

The second is such as]: "Slaughtering animals is bad."

---

٢٠٧   ومن الأسباب محبة التسالم والتصالح بإفشاء السلام وإطعام الطعام وقبح السب والتنفير وكفر النعمة، ومنها تأديب الشرائع لتكررها على الأسماع تستحسن كاستحسان الركوع والسجود، والتقرب بذبح الحيوان، ومنها الاستقراء للجزئيات الكثيرة فإن إفشاء السلام -مثلا- والصدق محمودان في أكثر الأوقات بالاستقراء -أي: تتبع الحوادث-، ولكنهما يقبحان عند قضاء الحاجة وعند السؤال عن رجل فاضل يراد قتله فهذان المقامان يقبح في إحداهما السلام، وفي ثانيها الصدق.

208   Al-Fādānī: Among the causes is the love for peace and reconciliation through spreading greetings of peace, offering food; and the repulsiveness of insults, alienation, and ingratitude. Another cause is the disciplining effect of religious laws due to their repetition in what is heard, making them regarded as good, such as the approval of bowing and prostration, and drawing near to Allah by sacrificing animals. Another cause is inductive reasoning from numerous particulars, as spreading peace and truthfulness, for example, are generally praiseworthy most of the time, according to induction (i.e. the successive observation of events). However, they become blameworthy in certain situations, such as during the fulfilment of bodily needs or when being asked about a virtuous man intended for killing. In these two cases, greetings of peace are inappropriate in the first, and truthfulness is blameworthy in the second.

The third is such as: "Approving of a wife's debauchery is dis-approved."

س   ما هي المُسلَّماتُ؟

ج   هـي مقدِّماتٌ مُسـلَّمةٌ عندَ النـاسِ، أو عندَ الخصمَينِ، كتسـليمِ
الفقهاءِ كَونَ الإجماعِ حُجّةً.

Q   What are *conceded premises* (*musallamāt*)?

A   They are the premises that people or the[ir] opponent concede. Such as the jurists (*fuqahā'*) conceding to consensus (*ijmā'*) being a binding proof (*ḥujjah*).

س   ما هو القياسُ الإقناعيُّ^(٢٠٩)؟

ج   هـو قيـاسٌ مؤلَّفٌ مِـن مُقدِّماتٍ مَقبولةٌ أو مَظنونةٌ، ويُسـمّى أيضًا
«خِطابيًّا».

Q   What is a *persuasive syllogism* (*qiyās iqnā'ī*)?[210]

A   It is a syllogism comprising premises that are plausible or presumed. It is also called *rhetorical* (*khiṭābiyyan*).

س   ما هي المَقبولاتُ؟

ج   هي مُقدِّماتٌ مَقبولةٌ مِن شخصٍ مُعتَقَدٍ فيه^(٢١١).

Q   What are *accepted premises* (*maqbūlāt*)?

A   They are premises accepted from an individual who is believed in [as a truthful authority].[212]

---

٢٠٩   والغرض منه: ترغيب الناس فيما ينفعهم من أمور معاشهم ومعادهم كما يفعله الخطباء والوعاظ.

210   Al-Fādānī: Its purpose is to encourage people towards what benefits them in their worldly affairs and the hereafter, just as preachers and admonishers do.

٢١١   بأن.كان له مزية وشرف موثوق به كجميع ما يتلقاه الناس عن الأساتذة والمعلمين والأباء بل أخبار الآحاد تجعل أدلة في علم الفقه.

212   Al-Fādānī: By it having a distinctive merit and a reliable honour, like all that people receive from teachers, educators, and parents; indeed, even single reports are considered evidence in the field of jurisprudence (*'ilm al-fiqh*).

س   ما هي المظنوناتُ؟

ج   هـي مُقدِّماتٌ يَحكُمُ بها العقلُ حُكمًا راجِحًا مع تجويزِ نَقيضِها، نحوُ: «كلُّ مَن يَطوفُ بالليلِ سارقٌ».

Q   What are the *presumed premises* (*maznūnāt*)?

A   They are premises the mind judges to be prepoderant while considering its contradictory equally possible. Such as "Everyone who walks around in the night is a thief."

س   ما هو القياسُ الشعريُّ[213]؟

ج   هو قياسٌ مؤلَّفٌ مِن مُقدِّماتٍ مُخيَّلةٍ.

Q   What is a *poetic syllogism* (*qiyās shiʿrī*)?[214]

A   It is a syllogism comprising premises that are imaginary.

س   ما هي المُخيَّلاتُ؟

ج   هي مُقدِّماتٌ تَنبسطُ مِنها النفسُ أو تنقبضُ، نحوُ: «الخمرُ ياقوتةٌ سيّالةٌ»؛ فتنبسطُ النفسُ وترغبُ في شُربها، ونحوُ: «العسلُ مِرَّةٌ[215] مُقَيَّئةٌ»؛ فتنقبضُ النفسُ وتَنقُرُ عنه.

Q   What are *imaginings* (*al-mukhayyilāt*)?

A   They are premises from which the soul is exhilarated or dejected. [They are] such as "Wine is liquid ruby," as the soul feels exhilaration and is drawn to drinking it. And such as "Honey

---

٢١٣   والغرض منه: انفعال النفس بالترغيب والترهيب.

214   Al-Fādānī: Its purpose is to influence the soul through encouragement and deterrence.

٢١٥   بكسر الميم ما في المرارة وهي هيئة لازمة بالكبد لكل ذي روح غير النعام والإبل.

is vomited bile (*mirrah*)[216]," as the soul feels dejection and is repulsed from it.

س ما هو القياسُ السوفُسطائيُّ^(٢١٧)؟

ج هو قياسٌ مؤلَّفٌ مِن مُقدِّماتٍ كاذبةٍ شـبيهةٍ بالحقِّ أو المشـهورِ أو مِن مُقدِّماتٍ وهميّةٍ.

Q What is a *sophistic syllogism* (*qiyās sūfusṭāʾī*)?[218]

A It is a syllogism comprising premises that are false [while] resembling the truth or what is commonly known, or [false] estimations.

س ما هي الوهميّاتُ؟

ج هـي مُقدِّمـاتٌ كاذبـةٌ يَحكُمُ بها الوهمُ في أمورٍ غيرِ مَحسوسةٍ، وهي لا تُفيدُ يقينًا ولا ظنًّا، بل مُجرَّدَ الشكِّ والشبهةِ الكاذبةِ، وإذا تُسـمّى أيضًا «مشـبَّهاتٍ»، نحوُ قولِنا في صورةِ فَرَسٍ على حائطٍ «هذا فرسٌ»^(٢١٩)؛ ونحوُ: قولِنا: «العقلُ نورٌ للناسِ^(٢٢٠)».

Q What are *false imaginings* (*wahmiyyāt*)?

A They are false premises asserted by the estimative [faculty] (*al-wahm*) in non-sensory matters. They do not provide certainty nor presumption, rather merely doubt and false resemblance. Hence, they are also called *deceptions* (*mushabbahāt*). Such as our statement concerning [i.e. a painting in] the form of a horse

---

216 Al-Fādānī: With a *kasrah* under the *mīm*, it refers to the bile, which is a condition inherent in the liver of every creature with a soul, except for ostriches and camels.

٢١٧ والغرض منه: التلبيس والمغالطة.

218 Al-Fādānī: Its purpose is to deceive and confuse.

٢١٩ فتقول في قياسها: «وكل فرس صهال» فـ «هذه الصورة صهال».

٢٢٠ فتقول في قياسها «وكل نور للناس فهو مرئي بالبصر» فـ «العقل مرئي بالبصر».

upon a wall: "That is a horse."[221] And such as our statement: "Reason is a light for people."[222]

---

221 Al-Fādānī: You would say in its syllogism: "And every mare is a whinnying one," so "this image is whinnying."

222 Al-Fādānī: You would say in its syllogism: "And every light for people is visible to sight," so "the intellect is visible to sight."

CLOSING

انتهت الرسالةُ بقلمٍ جامعِها ياسـينُ بنُ عيسـى الطالبُ بالسـنةِ الرابعةِ المتطوِّعةِ بدارِ العلومِ الدينيّةِ عامَ ١٣٥٤، والحمدُ لِلَّهِ ربِّ العالَمينَ.

The essay, penned by its compiler Yāsīn bin ʿĪsā, student in the fourth part-time year in Dār al-ʿUlūm al-Dīniyyah, ended in the year 1354 [AH/1945 AD]. And all praise is for Allah, Lord of the worlds. ❧

DETAILED TABLE OF CONTENTS

المُحْتَوَيَاتُ المفصلة

INDEX OF TECHNICAL TERMS

فهرس الاصطلاحات

Also from Islamosaic

Ark of Salvation

Connecting to the Quran

Etiquette with the Quran

Infamies of the Soul

Hadith Nomenclature Primers

Hanbali Acts of Worship

Ibn Juzay's Sufic Exegesis

Refutation of Those Who Do Not Follow the Four Schools

Sharḥ Al-Waraqāt

Shaykh al-Sulamī's Waṣiyyah

Supplement for the Seeker of Certitude

The Accessible Conspectus

The Encompassing Epistle

The Evident Memorandum

The Ultimate Conspectus